PRANAYAMA

A PATH TO HEALING AND FREEDOM

ALLISON GEMMEL LAFRAMBOISE

WITH YOGANAND MICHAEL CARROLL

Copyright © 2015 by Allison Gemmel Laframboise
All rights reserved.

Printed by CreateSpace, an Amazon.com Company

Available from Amazon.com and other retail outlets

Cover design by Vanessa Maynard
Swami Kripalu photograph from Kripalu Center for Yoga & Health
Headshot of Allison Gemmel Laframboise by Elaina Mortali
Headshot of Yoganand Michael Carroll by Jacci Gruninger
All other photographs by Chris Mastin and Yoganand Michael Carroll
Figures by Allison Gemmel Laframboise

For my sons, Kai and Tayo.
May you always pursue with fervor
that which makes you come alive.

- AMGL

To my students who inspire me with their practice,
and to Allison for the profound dedication
she has shown through creating this book.

- YMC

CONTENTS

Introduction..vii

Part I: Foundations of Pranayama

Chapter 1: Background..2

Chapter 2: Philosophy 14

Part II: Preparations for Pranayama

Chapter 3: Ideal Conditions for Pranayama.........76

Chapter 4: Shatkriyas 90

Chapter 5: Asana and Pranayama 114

Part III: The Practice of Pranayama

Chapter 6: Pranayama Techniques 124

Chapter 7: Mudras..221

Chapter 8: Working with Pranayama 259

Appendix: Daily Pranayama Practice Plans 266

Acknowledgments 274

About the Authors 276

Resources 278

INTRODUCTION

"You're fired."

I had just returned from a yoga retreat in Costa Rica, where I was staying in an open-air pagoda in the rainforest. The property could only be reached by boat, and when the trusty captain of my little dinghy delivered me from the sea to the beach, all I saw was sand and forest. No people. No buildings. No signs of civilization anywhere, until my brother came running out of the wall of trees to greet me, barefoot and waving both arms overhead.

The place was such a reprieve from the rest of life. Neither cell phones nor land lines existed there. In a couple of days, my body was completely in sync with the rhythms of the day. Absorbing the sounds of the wild all around us, we practiced yoga and learned to paint from a Shamanic artist. At night, there were lectures about local botanical life—a fascinating topic, but the teacher's style didn't captivate me. So I snuck a half mile down the beach to a tiny family-run hotel with an outdoor bar and patio, where I learned to dance salsa and merengue.

Having just come from the most enlivening, exhilarating, liberating, rejuvenating experience of my life, the news that I was being fired felt like a slap in the face. The job that had been snatched from me was Director of Special Projects at a public health research company near Boston. I had begun working there as a research assistant immediately after college. When I first started, I filed endless piles of paper and entered countless fields of data, which taught me a lot about research design, but I wanted to do much more. I worked hard to move up through the company of 200 employees, holding six different positions before landing my final role as a director.

Having always been an overachieving people-pleaser, I experienced getting fired as the ultimate failure in life. Not to mention that it felt incredibly unjust. From my perspective, it was a gross misunderstanding that could have been cleared up with a simple conversation. I was livid. I was heartbroken. I was mortified and ashamed.

And I was elated.

The morning I got the axe, I had turned to my brother on my way to work and said, "I'm ready for a change." I had started to feel stuck and uninspired in my job. Even though I loved the research topics, I felt as though we were spending exorbitant resources to *maybe* produce one or two findings that a handful of people *might* read in a scientific journal. I wanted to have an impact that I could see and feel firsthand.

Yet, I had been too comfortable to make a change on my own. I was making good money for a twenty-something, felt proud of my achievements, and was terrified to step out and try something new. Left to my own devices, I would have remained at that company for another decade. This was why, amidst my feelings of turmoil and chaos, part of me knew that this cosmic kick in the butt was exactly what I needed.

It was on that retreat in Costa Rica when I truly felt called to become a yoga teacher. Practicing yoga at least twice a day, free from my daily grind, I realized this practice needed to become a more integral part of my life. And I desperately wanted to share it with others. In fact, I felt responsible for doing so. I saw it as a way I could have that immediate influence I longed for, so different from the remote impact I might make in the research field.

Four years earlier, I had discovered Kripalu Yoga at a small studio in Brighton, Massachusetts, and this style of yoga resonated with me so deeply that I looked no further. My brother, after volunteering at Kripalu Center for Yoga & Health in Stockbridge, Massachusetts, told me, "If you go to Kripalu, you won't come back."

He was right. That fall after losing my job, I left Boston and headed to the Berkshires, where I began a 200-hour monthlong yoga teacher training (YTT) to become a Kripalu Yoga teacher.

I had no idea that I was about to begin a whole new life—meeting one man who would become my teacher, another who would become my husband, discovering the region that would become my new home, and incorporating my passions into a new career that would come to feel like my life's true calling.

I confess that, when I signed up to become a yoga teacher, I didn't want to take a training directed by Yoganand Michael Carroll, one of the YTT faculty members at the time. In fact, I tried hard to avoid him. I didn't know a thing about him, but all of my yoga teachers up to then had been women. Studying with women, I felt deeply nurtured by an unspoken connection to the feminine divine. I longed for that connection as I stepped through the doorway from practitioner to teacher. But Yoganand was teaching the next training offered at Kripalu, and the one after that felt too far away from my window of opportunity. So, despite my hesitations, I went for it.

By the middle of the first session, I found myself utterly intrigued by Yoganand's wisdom. "Yoga is not about being good. It's about being real and whole," he said. My mouth hung open. I had never heard such a concept within a spiritual tradition before, and it resonated with me deeply.

As the training continued, I became increasingly enthralled. Yoganand spoke of ancient and mysterious teachings in a way that I could apply to my own spiritual seeking. The content of these teachings resonated with me on a cellular level and a soul level as what felt like ultimate truth. I wanted to absorb it all—I couldn't scribble notes fast enough to capture this life-giving wisdom. I thought to myself, "I really hope this man has written some material that I can pore over later." Then I thought, "If he hasn't, I want to help him write it."

During the training, I approached Yoganand about the prospect of writing a book with him. He was pleasant in his response, but told me we should talk about it sometime after the training was over. He saw the realistic possibility that I was speaking from a grandiose place, drunk on yoga, and not necessarily grounded. I suspected he had been approached about such projects many times before.

I persisted. I attended a class that Yoganand held in Boston soon after my training and restated my strong desire to help translate his teachings into a more lasting form. Eventually, he agreed, and, three months after completing my 200-hour YTT, I moved to the Berkshires and spent the next two years with this book as my job. (It took another decade to fully complete the project, but that's its own story.)

I cut back my living expenses tremendously, taught a few yoga classes to pay my bills, and sat at my computer for hours every day. Just as I had felt called to become a yoga teacher, I felt it my duty in this life to transfer Yoganand's teachings onto paper.

As I immersed myself in the writing project, I continued advanced studies with Yoganand, diving headfirst into intensive retreats and teacher trainings. Under Yoganand's direction, I completed my 500-hour yoga teacher training and began to assist in his programs regularly. Eventually I trained with Yoganand to codirect an advanced pranayama program with him.

In my studies with Yoganand, I have had a number of deeply humbling and profound experiences. During one intensive retreat, Yoganand guided our group of 26 yogis through many of the techniques described in this book, along with other advanced practices from Swami Kripalu. We did this all day for one week straight. The intention was to raise our energy to high-enough levels that the protective armor we had built over time would soften. Then, we were to practice observing what rose to the surface once our guard was down. Some of the techniques seemed a bit strange to me, and some felt wildly bizarre, but I trusted Yoganand wholeheartedly, so I continually recommitted myself to my yoga. *Give yourself to the practice*, I told myself over and over. *Give yourself to the practice.*

Early on in the retreat, I began to feel very vulnerable. Then I came down with a cold, which made me feel even weaker. I chose to stay with it. *Give yourself to the practice.* I continued through the week, following Yoganand's guidance through yoga techniques that took me beyond my edge on many levels. I practiced watching, watching, watching my inner experiences unfold.

A number of times during the week, my thoughts returned to a letter I had received not long before: a rejection letter, telling me that an article I had submitted to a popular magazine had not been accepted. I couldn't understand why this was sticking with me. I had known when I submitted the article that it was highly unlikely to be accepted, so why was the letter lingering in my awareness? I simply observed the experience and my questions surrounding it.

"Interesting," I thought. Each time thoughts of the letter arose, they would fade before long, and something else would float into my mind.

During the final Friday-morning session of the retreat, Yoganand led us through a meditation to help us integrate the experiences of the week. Again, the rejection letter came into my mind, and I noticed a looming sense of failure surrounding it. This time, instead of passing on to something different, my thoughts were quickly followed by memories of being fired from the research company and feeling like a failure then as well. This opened up feelings of shame and self-loathing, which reminded me of how I felt as a child as a result of being sexually abused. I watched and watched and watched all of these experiences, thoughts, and feelings—guilt, hurt, anger, inadequacy, shame, and an acute sense of failure.

Without allowing these experiences to consume me, I watched from a still place within me, a place that had been developed and strengthened through my yoga. As I watched, I realized in amazement that all of these experiences related to shame and failure were closely linked. It was as if a spider web that had been in shadow was now moved into the light, and I could see how every silken thread connected to another. Thoughts about that rejection letter had been haunting me so relentlessly not because the letter itself was such a blow, but because those thoughts were linked to other experiences in my life that were excruciatingly painful. It wasn't that the old wounds were re-opened; rather, the fact that they had never fully healed was revealed to me.

After that final session, I left the retreat and spent the rest of the day alone. I wrote feverishly in my journal and spent time in nature. Sitting in the grass with those old wounds, I did nothing but simply acknowledge them. I had come to learn that sometimes acknowledging and witnessing my experience is far more powerful than analyzing, trying to figure it out or fix it. I was gentle with my pain and with myself. I made space for this internal storm of raw emotion to rage and then settle.

As challenging as it was to feel vulnerable and exposed to the pain of my old wounds, I felt an excitement and buzz from knowing I had done a significant piece of healing work during the retreat. I had gained tremendous clarity and self-knowledge, shining a floodlight on shadowy forces I didn't even know had been holding me back. Now I could do whatever was needed to help them heal further.

It turned out that little more was needed at the time. I had done years of prior work on some of those issues. Now, simply observing, being with, and acknowledging was enough. I felt empowered by knowing that this self-growth had happened by activating my own energies. I felt tremendous growth in my ability to remain steady as an observer of these soul-rattling feelings—not being consumed or owned by them, but allowing them to move within me and stir me up as I watched, steadfast and calm. I felt the validation of choosing yoga as my spiritual path and deciding to pack my bags and move to the Berkshires. I felt affirmed in trusting my instincts to *give myself to the practice*. Once the storm settled, I felt lighter and freer. By simply being seen and lovingly acknowledged, my old wounds had lost some of their hold on me, and I was able to walk on having shed much of their weight.

This is one of many profound experiences I have had studying with Yoganand, and one of the defining moments that led me to write this book. I share my story here to demonstrate that the practice of yoga can be a powerfully transformative spiritual path. Yoganand, informed by Swami Kripalu, teaches yoga in a way that supports and cultivates this deeper transformation.

What I admire most about Yoganand is the depth of his practice, combined with his refreshing relatability. He lived as a renunciate monk for 15 years, and spent as many years as a devoted husband. To this day, he maintains a physically, emotionally and spiritually rigorous yoga practice. His diverse life experiences allow Yoganand to share esoteric teachings in a way that is accessible for those of us who have never lived renunciate lifestyles or practiced eight hours of yoga every day.

Yoganand found tremendous wisdom in Swami Kripalu's teachings and has studied those teachings in great depth. He practices them in a deeply authentic way and then passes them on to other seekers. As his student, I appreciate the fact that he does not claim to have all the answers, but he generously shares the knowledge he has gained on his decades-long journey of exploring yoga.

Here I have gathered material from Yoganand's trainings and lectures, as well as recorded conversations between the two of us, over endless hours in person and by phone. I've translated Yoganand's verbal teachings into written word. It is my sincere hope that you will find inspiration and jewels of wisdom among these teachings that have profoundly informed my yoga and my life.

How to Get the Most from This Book

Yoga is an evolving art and science, and this book is written as a contribution to that continual emergence. It draws on ancient yogic teachings that can offer inspiration for the yoga we practice today. While we look back at the original techniques and early philosophies, this does not mean that there is a golden age to which we should return. Rather, we encourage contemporary yoga practitioners to continue moving forward, while remembering to look in the rearview mirror for guidance.

This text is an instructional guide, as well as a discussion about pranayama as an element of the tantric hatha yoga path. We examine the past to understand the present. We are part of an ever-evolving tradition and, to get the most out of it, it's helpful to have a complete understanding of what was done before us.

Yoganand

Philosophy becomes interesting when it means something. As a lifetime practitioner of yoga, I have benefited tremendously from looking at the history. Yoga has always changed. It's been very valuable for me to look at what yoga was in the past. Why is Kapalabhati pranayama the way it is? The answer is in the 14th century. Yoga has gone through a lot of changes. Whenever there's a change, that change is in the DNA forever. Yoga's history is so rich. To go back and be able to find pieces that enrich practice has helped me to understand and appreciate the power that yoga is.

It is profound to do a yoga technique, knowing that, thousands of years ago, yogis were practicing that very same technique. In some cases, we can draw upon the exact practices they did and learn from their intentions. In other cases, the techniques might not be safe or useful for our modern-day purposes, but we can still learn from the intention of these ancient practitioners, and draw on their inspiration and dedication.

In some sections of this book, we discuss techniques and practices that we don't recommend actually doing. So why bother including them at all? The yoga we are sharing comes from a specific lineage and tradition, and there's tremendous value in understanding the full picture of that tradition, even if the entirety of it doesn't apply to our practice today.

About Swami Kripalu

Mosquitoes swarmed the room as Swami Kripalu sat down to practice Anuloma Viloma, the only breathing technique he had learned from his master. Although his teacher had showered his student with yoga philosophy, he had passed on only one posture, one breathing exercise, and an assurance that, through the practice of these two things, he would learn everything he needed to know about yoga.

On this auspicious day in Halol, India, the swami began his breath work, and awareness of his body slipped away, as though he were drifting off to sleep. Suddenly, a wave of energy rose up his spine, his hand seemed to melt onto his lap, and his body trembled and shook. Without any conscious action, his arms and legs began to flail about, and rapid expulsions of breath pumped from within. As his body started to arch and writhe, he felt detached from himself, like a spectator watching the scene from afar. He had no time to anticipate what would happen next as the waves of energy and movement overcame him, so he simply watched.

After what might have been 10 minutes or what might have been an hour spent gazing at his own body squirming and thrashing about, Swami Kripalu collapsed into deep relaxation. When he awakened, he was shocked by the episode that had transpired both within his body and before his eyes.

At this point in his life, at age 38, Swami Kripalu had been practicing Anuloma Viloma three times each day, for 90 minutes before breakfast, lunch, and dinner. The next time he sat down to practice this pranayama, Bapuji (Sanskrit for "beloved father," as his students affectionately called him) was again astonished as his body exploded into a spontaneous flow of movement and breath as it had before. Soon, only one round of Anuloma Viloma triggered spontaneous movement and breath. As the days passed,

Swami Kripalu noticed the movements growing more intense and shifting to different parts of his body. Although he initially interpreted these events as illness or insanity, he trusted his teacher's guidance and continued his devout practice.

Eventually, a student brought Swami Kripalu a book on hatha yoga (the physical practice of yoga). The swami marveled when he realized that some of the classical yoga techniques in the text had occurred in his practice, even though he had never been taught them. He pored over posture books as he continued allowing his practice to unfold in this phenomenal, spontaneous manner.

It was in this way that the powerful practices of yogic breath work, known as pranayama, led Swami Kripalu into a deeply mystical side of yoga.

Numerous teachers, past and present, have mastered yoga postures, or asanas. Others excel as scholars of the yogic scriptures. Still others stand out as teachers of meditation or pranayama. Contemporary yoga master Swami Kripalu brought it all together.

A devoted yogi born in 1913 in the state of Gujurat, India, Haridas Majmundar met his guru in Bombay at the age of 19. The teacher initiated the young man into an advanced practice of yoga, which led to his profound energy awakening years later. Upon being initiated as a swami, Haridas received the name Kripalvanandaji, meaning "the bliss of God's grace," a name that was later shortened to Kripalu.

While Swami Kripalu studied the same yogic texts as everyone else, his intensive practices unveiled deep insights into the writings. In the course of his lifetime, he practiced hatha yoga for 10 hours a day for more than 30 years. This led him to see obvious meaning in passages that was not intuitive for others. He taught from this understanding, and built a model of yoga that is unique, mainly because of his unrivaled capacity to integrate the various and sometimes contradictory spheres of yoga.

Practices that seemed mysterious and vague, he rendered accessible. He took philosophies that appeared paradoxical and showed students how both could be true at different stages of practice. He authored volumes of material on technical practices like asana and pranayama, as well as philosophical commentaries on yogic scriptures. Swami Kripalu incorporated all of these realms into one comprehensive path which, to his followers, made perfect sense.

This great yogi's devotion and wisdom was the inspiration behind Kripalu Yoga, a tradition currently taught at Kripalu Center for Yoga & Health in Stockbridge, Massachusetts. At present, there are approximately eight thousand Kripalu-trained yoga teachers throughout the United States and around the world.

Yoganand

Finding Swami Kripalu's teachings so profound, I dove deeply into them during my 15 years as a resident of Kripalu. In the years after Swami Kripalu left his physical body in 1981, many of his valuable teachings have lost emphasis or have disappeared altogether. In order to revive those lost teachings, I developed the Pranakriya School for Yoga Healing Arts. I've also worked to integrate the teachings into programs currently offered through Kripalu's School of Yoga in my role as the school's Dean. The teachings in this book are true to the ancient tradition that Swami Kripalu lived and taught. I have adapted them from purely renunciate practices to techniques accessible to Western students living active lives in the world.

Two Paths of Hatha Yoga

Long ago in the history of yoga, a division occurred in which yoga schools split themselves into two paths. Down one road traveled yogis who saw the body as an object to be transcended and discarded. To them, human flesh was an obstacle at best and a prison at worst. These yogis sought "out of the body" enlightenment. Practitioners worked to subdue and control the senses, body, and mind, so their souls could abandon human existence and merge with spirit. To them, liberation happened outside of the body. Yoga scholar Georg Feuerstein, in his book *The Yoga Tradition*, calls this path the *verticalist* path; the direction these yogis wanted to travel was in, up, and out of their bodies.

The other path attracted yogis who revered the body and mind as complicated puzzles to solve. These yogis recognized energies inside the body that could be activated and harnessed to dissolve the ego mind and allow the soul to experience universal oneness. Disciples of this path sought "in the body" enlightenment, diving into their bodies to liberate their souls. Feuerstein labeled this path the *horizontalist* path.

Both the horizontalist and verticalist paths extend back beyond recorded time. Some evidence suggests that the horizontalist path evolved from shamanism in rural areas, where people saw the cycles of life everywhere and could not think of existence outside them. The same evidence implies that the verticalist path developed in urban areas where practitioners wished to create sterile environments to contain the messiness of embodied existence.

As modern practitioners, we seldom experience the split between the paths of out-of-the-body enlightenment and in-the-body enlightenment. The hatha yoga traditions have blended together, and we each take the pieces that fit our worldviews and individual purposes for practicing yoga. The distinction, however, remains crucial in the study of pranayama, yogic meditation, and other deeper practices of yoga.

With pranayama, for instance, the verticalist schools use the breath to build concentration and avoid disturbance. On the horizontalist path, pranayama is used to intensify aliveness and reveal the truth of the yogi's body, thoughts, and feelings. Once she becomes aware of this truth, the yogi is challenged to integrate it so that she can live from an awareness of her whole self.

Pranakriya Yoga and Kripalu Yoga are both horizontalist paths at their roots. In his book *Asana and Mudra*, Swami Kripalu states that there are between 400 and 600 pranayamas, which is a testament to the complexity of pranayama on a horizontalist path. Thus, the teachings in these pages originate from the perspective of the path of in-the-body enlightenment.

Ancient Hatha Yoga Texts

For our purposes, the phrase "ancient yoga" refers to the form of the practice beginning around the 12th and 13th centuries, when hatha yoga became distinct from other forms of yoga, and continues through the beginning of the British domination of India, around the 18th century. During this period, the three most important classical hatha yoga texts were written: The *Hatha Yoga Pradipika*, the *Gheranda Samhita* and the *Shiva Samhita*.

The *Hatha Yoga Pradipika*, written by the yogi Svatmarama around the 14th century, describes four main areas of yoga practice: asana, pranayama, mudra, and meditation. This foundational scripture provides the nuts and bolts of yoga practice, describing specific techniques and instructions on how to do them.

The *Shiva Samhita* and *Gheranda Samhita* cover the same material as the *Hatha Yoga Pradipika*, while expanding into other realms of yoga. The *Shiva Samhita* adds a chapter on philosophy, and the *Gheranda Samhita*, written in the 17th century, elaborates extensively on advanced yoga practices, such as the shatkriyas and mudras, both of which are discussed in later chapters of this book.

While the above three texts describe yoga in raw technical terms, the *Bhagavad Gita* is completely allegorical. It focuses heavily on philosophy, using metaphorical narrative to explain what the practices feel like from inside the yogi. Swami Kripalu viewed the *Bhagavad Gita* as the perfect guide for hatha yoga practice. It does not tell the yogi which postures to do, but rather describes the emotional and energetic experiences for which the yogi should reach while doing postures.

All of the original texts require interpretation. For one, they are too concise to stand alone. Furthermore, they are written in Sanskrit, a language in which words have multiple meanings. To interpret the *Bhagavad Gita*, one can look at all the definitions of each word and fit them together like harmonics to understand what the authors were trying to convey. More challenging to unravel are texts like the *Hatha Yoga Pradipika*, *Gheranda Samhita* and *Shiva Samhita*. These three texts were written in a code language called *Sandhya Basya*, meaning "twilight language." *Sandhya Basya* is intentionally confusing. It looks like very poor Sanskrit and was used to keep the teachings secret.

That the three technical texts were written in a code language renders them vague. They do not make sense in the way the *Bhagavad Gita* does. It is obvious that something is purposely hidden. For example, the scriptures say that a yogi who masters the technique called *Kechari mudra* "can eat the flesh of a cow and drink wine and still remain pure." The texts are riddled with symbols and metaphors, which make it impossible to fully understand the message unless you know the secret language.

Not knowing the code language, we will never know exactly what the authors intended. To get the most out of these texts, however, we can approach the verses in the ancient texts as mosaic tiles, piecing them together with additional information from three valuable sources: a teacher, such as Swami Kripalu, who practiced and wrote from his personal realization; our own personal practices; and study of the original texts. Study alone is not enough, because much of the written material is counterintuitive. By adding sincere practice to your study, insights come. Those insights become new tiles in the mosaic that can help to complete a vibrant picture that refines itself as we continue to study and practice.

This book is informed by Swami Kripalu's practice and writings as well as Yoganand's personal practice and study of the scriptures and the horizontalist traditions. It is our hope that you will combine it with insights from your own yogic endeavors to create a new mosaic that is yours alone. These teachings descend from a long tradition of exploration into a spiritual unknown. We encourage you to keep the mystery alive. Ideally, you will learn enough to enrich your practice and find inspiration to delve sincerely into it. When you do this, the mystery will unfold on its own.

The Sanskrit Language

One of the earlier Indo-European languages, Sanskrit remains the language of yoga and Hinduism today. Dating back to 1500 BCE, Sanskrit was spoken in the culture from which yoga emerged, and it is the tongue from which most modern north Indian languages derive.

Although many yogic terms still appear in Sanskrit, the language, like Latin, is considered a "dead" language, meaning it is no longer spoken, except in small religious communities. Because Sanskrit is obsolete in everyday use, it is ideal for propagating spiritual teachings throughout the centuries. All viable languages are continually evolving, so the definitions of words shift. With a dead language, words hold their meanings indefinitely, making it far more conducive to preserving original knowledge through time and space.

We commonly see different English spellings of Sanskrit words. This is because the Sanskrit alphabet contains 52 letters, twice as many as the English alphabet. As words have been translated from Sanskrit to English over the past century, different transliteration schemes have been used. For example, the word *Sankhya*, describing a school of yogic thought, is sometimes spelled *Samkhya*, because in Sanskrit the sound falls somewhere in between the English M and N.

A common source of variation is the presence or absence of a vowel at the end of a translated Sanskrit word.

For example, you may encounter *sahit kumbhak* or *sahita kumbhaka*. Sanskrit texts were often meant to be sung, and Sanskrit words frequently ended in vowels to support their melodic quality. Most modern Indian languages based on Sanskrit have dropped the ending vowels. Swami Kripalu, like many Indian teachers, would often begin lectures using the traditional pronunciation of Sanskrit words, then progress to using modern variations of the words within a few minutes.

This means there is not one universally correct way to spell Sanskrit words in English. If you find words spelled differently in another source, it does not mean that one is right and the other wrong, but simply that different translations were used.

In this book, the first use of a Sanskrit word is italicized for emphasis, with subsequent usages appearing in standard type to make the text more readable.

What is the Goal of Liberation?

Enlightenment and liberation, often conflated with the Judeo-Christian concept of salvation, are vague concepts to most modern practitioners. In some yoga texts and traditions, the enlightened master leaves his body and becomes one with the universe or God. In other traditions, the enlightened yogi lives as a *Jivan mukti*, or liberated soul, for the duration of his natural life, leaving behind legends of miracles and profound wisdom.

Many yoga texts tell of a liberated master who transforms his body into an immortal or divine container that does not grow old, and then lives forever as a servant of God, sometimes disappearing for long periods of time and then reappearing in a different form as a great teacher or prophet. This concept of an enlightened yogi is very similar to the idea of the *Bodhisattva* in *Mahayana Buddhism*.

Swami Kripalu held the latter view, and spoke of his teacher, who he believed had achieved a divine body thousands of years ago. This master, whom he called Swami Pranavanandji, appeared to Swami Kripalu when he was 19 years old. He performed many miracles that inspired his young students to practice with great vigor, with the goal of obtaining divine bodies of their own.

The divine body forms when a yogi raises the energy in his body to an extremely high level and holds it there for a very long time. The strong Prana (energy, or life force) heals the body and then slowly transforms it. This process is sometimes called "baking the pot." When unbaked, the pot, or body, melts in water, meaning the yogi ages with time. Once baked, however, the pot does not change when submerged in water, meaning the yogi does not age.

Yoganand

My belief is this: If you are enlightened, you will know it. If you are not enlightened, you probably cannot know what it is like and probably should not restrict it to a description apprehensible to the mind. I do not claim to be there. At the same time, my practice has progressed me toward greater spiritual freedom. There is a path up a mountain that I have been exploring for many years, but I have not reached the top, and I am not going to surmise what you will find if you do.

PART I

FOUNDATIONS OF PRANAYAMA

CHAPTER ONE
BACKGROUND

What is Pranayama?

"Prana is the thread which unites body, mind and atman [the self] in the form of a garland of flowers." —Swami Kripalu, from *Bapuji on Kripalu Yoga*

Inhale deeply. Now exhale through your mouth with a gentle "Ahhhh." You have just practiced a simple yet profound *pranayama*—the sigh.

The Sanskrit word pranayama combines *Prana*, meaning both air and aliveness, and *yama*, meaning restraint. Pranayama can also be divided into *Prana* and *ayama*, which means to lengthen or increase.

Whereas some texts restrict the definition of Prana to spiritual energy or breath, **Swami Kripalu saw Prana as everything that is an expression of aliveness.** Just as clay is the raw material that forms a flowerpot, Prana is the substratum woven by the mind to create thoughts, feelings, and sense perceptions. It also inspires the body to perform actions. Another way to conceptualize Prana is as pure energy, without any labels.

Since Prana has essentially two definitions—breath and aliveness—**the term pranayama also carries two meanings.** The first definition involves the **yogic techniques used to restrain or deepen the breath**, such as the ones that led Swami Kripalu to new spiritual awareness. The second definition refers to **the process of enhancing the flow of aliveness**, or inhibiting the flow of aliveness from its normal direction.

Figure 1. Two definitions of pranayama

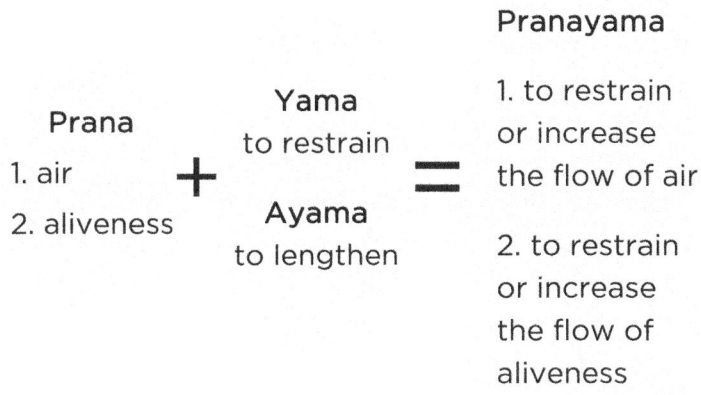

What does it mean to "inhibit the flow of aliveness"? From a yogic perspective, a wealth of energy continually flows through our bodies and minds. We often channel that energy outward where it adheres to people, things, and situations. We then incorporate those objects into our views of the world and our views of ourselves.

Imagine walking out of the grocery store and seeing a luxurious new car. As you admire the perfect, shiny vehicle, you realize you would love to have one yourself. You energetically link yourself to the beautiful new car and your perception of the situation becomes skewed by desire. If you then work hard to save money to buy the car, your identity suddenly shifts, and you become the driver and owner of a fancy new car.

When energy binds to things, such as money, a new car, or a computer, we call it obsession. When energy binds to people, such as family, friends, or lovers, we call it codependence. These are both forms of attachment. The goal of pranayama is to shift that process. Restraining the life force can help us disconnect from objects and situations that drain our energy, so we can keep the energy inside instead, where it increases our aliveness.

Here's another example: You reach the end of a long, hard Friday at work. Ecstatic for the arrival of the weekend, you feel completely liberated by the time you leave the office at five o'clock. You ask yourself what to do next. Ice cream comes to mind. You start craving it intensely and, before you know it, your energy focuses on nothing but where to get a pint of ice cream. You remember the convenience store on the way home carries it. At home, you grab a spoon, land in your favorite chair, shovel the Super Fudge Deluxe Chunk into your mouth, and feel peaceful and calm again.

We constantly find ways to "dump" our extra energy and return to a comfort zone. When you left work, you experienced a heightened level of energy that felt uncomfortable. You ran to the convenience store for ice cream because you needed to squelch that anxious energy. Once the energy was subdued, you felt at ease once again. This is how we manage our life-force energy, usually without even realizing it.

The ancient yogis took a different approach. **They welcomed intensity and practiced living in a state of heightened energy.** They became comfortable with it over time and could therefore live with more vibrancy and vitality.

Another way to understand the effect of energy levels is to think of a day when you awoke, and getting out of bed felt unbearable. Life felt menacing, and you could barely get yourself into the shower. Now think of a day when you sprang out of bed, ready to tackle the world. What was different between the two days? Energy. On the daunting day, your energy was extremely low. On the bountiful day, your energy was high. **This invisible force called energy influences all our perceptions; by changing the energy, the perceptions shift as well.**

I watch my students come into a yoga class, and I visualize a string connected to each person's head, stretching back out the door. The string could be connected to a thought about a meeting earlier in the day, or a question: "Is my car safe where I parked it?" As I lead meditation and pranayama, I like to think of myself as energetically walking around with big scissors and snipping the strings so my students can let go and be present.

Pranayama techniques help us detach from the objects that devour our energy; when this happens, endless possibilities reveal themselves. When we unplug from the known, an unknown opens. A mystery unfolds, and we realize we are not who we thought we were. It's similar to when you take a week off from your daily grind and, in the middle of vacation, you look back at who you were in the midst of that stressful world of work and ask yourself "Who *was* that person?"

The ancient yogis wanted to disconnect because they saw the world as a trap. Whether or not we feel that way about the world, **yoga can open us to the fullness of our potential, helping us to live in a way that is abundantly radiant and vibrantly alive.**

History of Pranayama

According to the ancient yogis, there is a whole universe of experience within every human being, but we often shrink from that full realm of existence because it's too intense. **The practice of pranayama connects us with the full range of what we are feeling.** Here's one story of how pranayama came to be:

In prehistoric times, a caveman, walking barefoot through the jungle, exclaimed with uncontrollable glee, "Life is sweet!" He gazed at the sunrise, the birds bursting with vibrant hues of red, yellow, and blue, and the lush green trees shading the forest from the rising sun. He rounded the bend and a glorious waterfall stopped him in his tracks. "Wow!" he exclaimed. Crystal-clear water cascaded from the mountain, creating tiny prisms and rainbows in its mist. With the earth pressing gently between his toes, he felt completely at one with nature. Relishing the sweetness of this magnificent morning, he bent down to pick a plump berry from a shrub.

All of a sudden, Mr. Caveman heard the growl of a saber tooth tiger behind him. He yelled, "Oh my God! He's going to eat me!" Then, he gathered himself and said, "Wait a minute. If I fall apart, he *will* eat me. I must hold myself together." He tightened his body and squashed the intense emotions evoked by the tiger's growl. The caveman used his rational mind to analyze the situation: "The tiger's growl came from behind me, so I will go left." He took two steps to his left, then remembered, "No, the mountain to the west will slow me down." He devised an alternate plan. "I know a pass to the east. If I go that direction, I will get away." Moments later, he found himself safe and sound and thought, "Phew! I got away! If I had remained open and upset, the tiger would have eaten me. But I shut down my emotions and escaped. I will remember this."

At the end of the day, the sun began to sink behind the lush landscape, and the caveman decided he should head home. As he neared his cave, he remembered, "Uh oh. I forgot to take the garbage out this morning." Knowing how it infuriated his cavewoman when he fell short of his responsibilities, his mind made a connection: *Cavewoman = saber tooth tiger = threat.*

Remembering how he had survived the tiger earlier in the day, he thought to himself, "I better tighten up." So he tensed his body, thinking he would get bombarded when he walked through the front door of the cave. He not only tightened up to avoid being attacked, but also to avoid feelings of guilt and shame for disappointing his beloved cavewoman. Finding it much simpler to shut down all of his feelings, he went inside to eat his dinner.

Meanwhile, inside the cave, Mrs. Cavewoman paced anxiously between the den and the kitchen, feeling slighted and disrespected because her husband had failed to take the garbage out that morning. Noticing these feelings, she told herself to push them away. "Even though this hurts, and I know he might do it again, I just want to ignore the fact that I feel disappointed. I want to have a peaceful evening with my husband."

"Oh, hello, dear. How was your day?" she asked her husband with a pleasant smile on her face.

"It was fine, thank you," he politely responded. "Is dinner ready?"

"Yes, we're having mammal steaks tonight."

"Oh great, my favorite!"

With that, they sat down to a quiet meal together. On the surface, life felt peaceful. But, underneath the pleasantries, raw emotions boiled.

This tale illustrates one theory about how pranayama evolved: **Somewhere along the line, humans learned to diminish feelings so we could function rationally.** The process began as a survival mechanism, such as the caveman escaping the saber tooth tiger by shutting down his fears. **Over time, this safety device evolved into a way of living in the world.** Just as the caveman squashed his emotions to keep peace with his wife, we have learned that suppressing our feelings makes everything flow more smoothly. Had we not learned to squash strong feelings, we would still be in the jungle beating each other with clubs. Because we can squash intensity and smile, everything seems okay. Then we go home and find some place to release the emotion by eating a pint of ice cream, drinking a six-pack of beer, or spending hours on the internet.

The ancient yogis noticed their lives becoming more muted and said, "Something is missing. The sunrise appears less vibrant than before. Food tastes blander than before. I notice myself aging faster. Something seems wrong." These realizations led them to look for ways to return to an unrepressed state. The techniques they discovered in India were called yoga. Many of the practices centered around the breath, and became known as pranayama. **Thus, at a foundational level, pranayama helps us reconnect with what we actually feel, beneath the veil of what we** *think* **we feel**. In connecting us to our true emotions, pranayama exposes the raw, unfiltered, luminous truth of who we really are.

Why Pranayama Has Been Marginalized

When we think of modern yoga traditions, we tend to picture yogis flowing through postures. Although breath work goes hand in hand with the postures, we are less likely to envision a group of practitioners sitting down to breathe, even though some ancient yoga schools focused exclusively on pranayama.

Why, then, did pranayama get sidelined? There are two main reasons. First, modern practitioners typically come to yoga for athletic or health purposes. They want to increase their strength and flexibility, lower their stress levels, or improve their ability to relax. They might have no desire to feel more of their inner experiences. Second, most people today approach yoga as a practice, not a path. They focus on the practice they are doing now and the effects it is generating. **Ancient yogis saw yoga as a layered path.** Their approach was: "What I am doing now is preparing me for what I cannot practice now, but will someday be able to practice through my current actions."

Imagine living in India two thousand years ago. If you set out to learn yoga, you would not see a sign for the Bombay Yoga Studio as you walked down the street. Yoga was hidden. If you wanted to find it, you had to look hard.

You had to go into seedy bars and talk to people on the street. You might find someone with connections to a yoga school, but that didn't mean you would get in.

If, eventually, a teacher accepted you as a yoga student, you joined a mystery school with many layers of initiation into a spiritual technology. The master might give you a simple asana routine and tell you to practice *yamas* and *niyamas* (the ethical guidelines laid out in the ancient yoga texts). You practiced those for a while. Then, as the teacher felt that you were ready, he would say "*Psst!* Come over here. There's another level I want to tell you about," and he would initiate you into the next level of practice.

These endless layers of practice often seemed to contradict each other. Imagine this scenario: You join a yoga school, and the master says, "Here is a series of 40 asanas. I want you to practice it every single morning, and hold each asana for a full minute."

"But I can't hold it for a minute!" you respond.

"Well, practice until you can. But don't miss one day. If you do, you cannot be part of this school."

You spend three years practicing your intense asana routine every single morning, holding each posture for one minute. This type of practice builds tremendous strength and will.

One day, the teacher comes to you and says, "You are doing very well. Stop that practice completely. Go practice these pranayamas."

You say, "But I like my asanas!"

"No, you are done with them. Those asanas have already given you all that they were meant to give you. Go practice these pranayamas."

Because you have done all that asana work, your body is open. The pranayamas will be more effective than if you had not spent all that time on the asanas. Pranayama affected ancient yogis differently than it does modern practitioners, because the ancients did layers of preparatory work.

You do the pranayama for a long time, and your energy begins to soar. You acclimate to the elevated energy. Then the teacher says, "See these five asanas? I want you to go into that room, and hold the first asana for 10 minutes."

You protest: "I'll die if I hold it for 10 minutes!"

"Hold it for 10 minutes, then completely relax, and let your body move any way it wants to move for 10 minutes. Then do the next asana."

You just moved into a surrender practice that contradicts the earlier willful practice, in which you held each asana for one minute.

After a while, the teacher says, "You're doing great. You're ready for the next level."

These layers of practice characterized ancient yoga. Within the layers were meditation, intense willful practice, asana, pranayama, and surrender yoga. Swami Kripalu called his deepest teachings the "yoga secrets." According to Swami Kripalu, the yoga secrets were only to be given to those who met specific criteria and were sworn to secrecy when they received them. Many old yoga texts support this view. The *Bhagavad Gita*, for example, ends with the teacher instructing the graduating student, Arjuna, not to "speak of this to one who is without austerity, or one who is without devotion." (Bhagavad Gita 18:67)

Often, then, students did not even know the deeper layers existed until they were ready for them. Each stage guided the yogi through a precise spiritual technology to liberation.

Quite likely, at one point in time, only one yoga school existed, and it encompassed all of the layers. Why, then, are there so many diverse yoga paths today? Suppose a student in the very first yoga school worked hard for many years, moving through 10 layers of practice. Then he said, "I understand these teachings. I'm going to leave and start my own school." As he walked away, his teacher said, "I was just about to teach him the eleventh layer." The student then started his own school, teaching all that he knew, but his ability to disseminate the original teachings went only as far as his studies with his master had progressed.

Swami Kripalu said that, in a lifetime, a teacher might initiate only two or three students into some of the deeper levels of yoga, because only that many would come along who were ready to learn them. What if, in a particular teacher's lifetime, no students came along who were ready for a certain teaching? What if the teacher died before anyone was prepared to learn the most advanced techniques? Political situations— wars, social upheavals, and economic crises—also caused yoga schools to fragment. **Thus, over the course of time, many yoga traditions simplified.**

When Swami Kripalu came to America, he taught a path with about five layers. At the time, he worked intensely with surrender yoga, the aspect of his practice that most impressed his senior disciple. This senior student then walked away to found his own school with three layers and a strong focus on surrender yoga, without looking at the willful work that Swami Kripalu had done before surrender yoga.

This is one of countless situations where a student carried forward a piece of what he had been taught— maybe a big piece, but still only a piece—and left the rest behind. When students carried one aspect of their teachers' knowledge forward, something was lost.

In many modern yoga schools in the West, asana has become the exclusive or primary focus. While asana was part of the original yoga technology, it was not the only component. A yogi learned asana, benefited from it, and then moved on. Maybe he incorporated pranayama into his asana, then asana faded into the background while pranayama moved to the forefront. Or asana, other than seated positions, completely disappeared, and pranayama evolved into a meditation path. **Although they were meant to be bridges to more advanced practices, techniques like asana have become islands.**

Yoganand

Because of these lost pieces and fragmentations, I firmly believe in studying from as many schools as you can. Get pieces from different sources, and weave them together. I do not believe we will ever rebuild that original yoga school. Too many pieces have been lost. If we can grasp the original intention of a practice, however, we can approach yoga in a way that recreates that intention. I teach pranayama according to an intention that I learned from Swami Kripalu, which I also found reinforced in the ancient texts.

Therefore, when the technical descriptions in the texts are vague, I do the pranayamas in ways that meet the broader intention. This is the best way I have found to recapture the essence of the original teachings and build on their riches to deepen my understanding, practice, and teaching of yoga today.

CHAPTER TWO
PHILOSOPHY

In this chapter, we will look at several models for understanding energy and pranayama, and we'll use a master diagram to tie it all together for you. Let's get started.

Building a Self

A person drowning in a river sees a log and grabs onto it. Another log comes along, and he grabs that one too. He ties them together, collects anything else that floats by, and builds a raft upon which he can float. That raft becomes his ground and his safety, without which he would die.

In a similar way, **humans are born into an ocean of chaotic sensory experience.** We see lights and colors, feel sensations, and hear sounds with no ability to make sense of them. We move from the warm, serene environment of the womb into the cold, bright world of the delivery room, and we have no clue what is happening. Our minds have not developed yet. We can only respond to impressions. Like a drowning man who thrashes and flounders before building a survival raft, we cannot even control the movements of our bodies. Consider the newborn baby: His legs wiggle and his arms flail. He yells and cries. He has no mind.

According to yogic philosophy, having no idea who we are is a terrifying state. Just as the drowning man grabs logs to build a raft, the newborn soul begins absorbing data from the external world to construct a sense of self. Like the raft, the sense of self becomes one's foundation and security.

The identity born of this data-gathering process is called the *ahankara*, literally meaning "self shape" or "self activity." The ahankara roughly equates to the ego in western psychology, except that the ego sometimes takes on a negative connotation in spiritual or religious traditions, whereas ahankara is neutral.

Consider this example of building an ahankara: An infant starts looking for facts to figure out who he is. His mother scoops him up and says, "Oh, Daniel, my darling little baby boy, I'm so happy to be your mother. I love you." The baby just learned five things about himself: (1) he is Daniel; (2) he is a boy; (3) he is a baby; (4) the woman holding him is his mother; and (5) she loves him. **Our ahankaras are made up of all the things that people tell us about ourselves, messages that we interpret about ourselves, and lessons we learn from our successes and failures.**

Through the teenage years, the ahankara strengthens, although some vulnerable cracks remain. Tremendous insecurity surrounds those cracks.

Yoganand

My first job was at a Tastee Freez soft-serve ice cream shop. Being young with no work experience, I felt lost, insecure, and overwhelmed with self-doubt. I went into the job thinking, "I'm not sure I can do this." Such concerns led me to question what it would mean if I could not do it. Would it make me a bad person? Would it indicate that I did not belong? Would it prevent me from ever being successful in the world?

As we first build our ahankaras, we have no solid ground on which to stand, and the possibility of a fracture in one's self-sense can feel devastating. By our 20s and 30s, our ahankaras solidify. We have careers. We are doctors. We are teachers. Maybe we have families. We know who we are. Our ahankaras are strong, so we hold onto them, and we resist any changes that threaten them.

Building an ahankara is like a bird building a nest. She uses whatever she finds: twigs, leaves, newspaper scraps, cigarette butts. **Since our ahankaras consist of everything people have told us about ourselves in addition to our interpretations of our experiences, some parts of our ahankaras are likely flawed and inaccurate.**

Yoganand

When I was about 11 years old, my father told me I was lazy. He had assigned me a task, and I joked that the task was beneath my dignity. He took my joke seriously and turned away from me. Many years later, in a personal growth workshop, I realized I was still working long hours to convince my father I was not lazy. I had incorporated his message into my ahankara as truth, and that message was partially dictating the course of my life.

The bird's nest analogy illustrates how ahankara forms. Once formed, ahankara is held together by our need for certain ideas and beliefs to be true. **The more we need something to be true, the stronger that aspect of ahankara becomes.**

Yoganand

As a yoga teacher, I have studied and practiced numerous postures, and I know the Sanskrit names for many of them. At a workshop, a student asked me the name of a posture, and my mind went blank. It seemed wrong that I didn't know. I felt upset and, for a moment, I perceived that student as an enemy. Not knowing posture names threatened my ahankara. It felt like I was flawed, not what I thought I was and not who I felt I needed to be. This encounter reminded me that the "I am a yogi" part of my ahankara carries a huge charge.

By contrast, I took a walk in the woods with a friend from another state. He asked me the name of a plant growing along the path, and I said, "I don't know," without giving it a second thought. No aspect of my ahankara needs me to know the names of local weeds. My ahankara wasn't threatened in this situation, so the charge was barely there.

What is woven into our ahankaras and the charge associated with it influences our experiences tremendously. Our ahankaras tell us how much happiness, love, and success we deserve. We need our ahankaras as desperately as drowning men need their rafts, so we hold them close.

Two Stages of Yoga

Yoga can be viewed in two stages with regard to ahankara. **The first stage is purifying ahankara.** Purifying ahankara basically means removing the litter from the bird's nest— extracting the gross distortions so that ahankara can function optimally.

Yoganand

Many times at the end of a pranayama practice, I have felt worthless. Part of me wanted to believe this feeling of uselessness and spiral into self-loathing. Another part of me said, "Wait a minute. I am okay." I recognized that an emotion was activated by my pranayama, but it was not reality. I sat back, and instead of reacting to the worthlessness, I objectively watched it until it passed. In so doing, my ahankara healed a bit.

Purifying ahankara, then, means raising energy through practices such as pranayama, so that ahankara softens. When ahankara softens, it can heal or shift.
    Here is another way to think about purifying ahankara. As complex human beings, we often have opposing voices within us. The opposing voices result in conflicts that are like a bunch of little energy storms swirling around inside of us. Those little storms create such a mess

that we feel a need to contain them, so we encapsulate them, forming knots or cysts in our ahankaras. Those storms can last a lifetime, and carrying them consumes energy, just like holding a beach ball under water consumes energy. If we relax, it will pop right up to the surface.

> # Stage One
> Purifying ahankara means raising energy through pranayama so that ahankara can soften and heal.

When the yogi enters the meditation room and practices pranayama, he raises the energy in his nervous system. The extra energy softens ahankara by reducing the yogi's need to be stable and, if the energy is high enough, ahankara starts to dissolve. When ahankara starts to dissolve, the little energy storms appear. Although the yogi might feel afraid or excited, the goal is to sit back and watch, without reacting. A yogi with a history of trauma might see this storm:

My uncle never should have done that to me.
But he did do that to me.
I must have deserved it.
I didn't deserve it.

One voice says, "I am the scum of the earth." Another voice says, "I am okay." **If the yogi watches the voices interact without feeding either of their charges, they will cancel each other out and dissipate.** Then, when the energy subsides and ahankara reforms, it can reform without that storm. That is purification of ahankara.

The second stage in yoga is dissolving ahankara completely. To the ancients, the ahankara was not real; it was an energy phenomenon. They worked to dissolve ahankara in order to melt into oneness with spirit, God, and all of creation. They wanted to come to a place where they could say, "I do not exist, other than as an energy phenomenon." To them, a yogi was no different from a tree, a flower, or a sunrise.

When ahankara is dissolving, yoga can feel rapturous. Asana and pranayama practice generates currents of ecstasy in the body and mind. The yogi finds himself dissolving into bliss for timeless moments during meditation. And, for a short time after the practice, the yogi often finds himself melting into whatever object, person, or scene he encounters. The dissolving of ahankara can be very sweet or, like the purifying of ahankara, it can be terrifying.

> **Stage Two**
>
> Dissolving ahankara means raising energy high enough that the yogi melts into oneness with creation.

The *Bhagavad Gita* recounts a dialogue between a student and his teacher on a battlefield. **Swami Kripalu believed that the battle represented the process of purifying and dissolving ahankara.** He also believed the series of questions the student asked the teacher were questions that would arise in every seeker going through the process of purifying and dissolving ahankara.

Twice in the Bhagavad Gita, the student, Arjuna, becomes overwhelmed and cries out to his teacher for help. In Chapter 1, Arjuna realizes that all of the soldiers in both armies are his relatives. Digesting the fact that countless loved ones will die, he turns to his teacher and pleads to be released from fighting. **The teacher, Krishna, instructs Arjuna to fight with detachment.**

The battle represents the process of healing old hurts. The relatives who must die are the coping systems we cling to in order to maintain the wounded ahankara. Krishna's direction to fight is the conviction that a yogi must do the difficult work to heal and become more whole.

In Chapter 11 of the *Bhagavad Gita*, Arjuna asks Krishna to grant him the vision of God. Krishna agrees, and Arjuna finds it blissful, until he notices his own sense of purpose dissipating (ahankara dissolving). He begs Krishna to take the vision away, but instead, **Krishna encourages Arjuna to cultivate understanding and devotion to endure the truth.** This is encouragement for the yogi to cultivate a strong capacity to see his or her own truth.

Although these stages of purifying and then dissolving ahankara are presented as sequential, the two processes are actually intermingled. A practitioner might experience a bit of purification and healing, followed by a taste of dissolving, then some more purification. **The pain of purifying ahankara is often offset by the sweetness of dissolving ahankara**, where one begins to melt and let go. This is simply the process of growing or evolving. The *Bhagavad Gita* calls this process *swadharma*, the duty one is born to, or the action that arises within the individual on the path to wholeness.

Even though purifying and dissolving ahankara happens concurrently, traditional teachers encouraged one or the other, depending on the student. To a student with family responsibilities, a teacher would give postures, pranayamas and meditations that would cultivate sensitivity to the body and emotions. These would support purifying ahankara. For a renunciate student, a skilled teacher would assign techniques to raise energy to very high levels, encouraging the dissolving of ahankara.

For modern yogis functioning in the world, purifying ahankara is the appropriate phase of yoga on

which to focus. Dissolving ahankara completely is not practical for those of us who have jobs, families, and responsibilities. To us, a yogi with no ahankara would look crazy. Many mythological and historical stories describe advanced yogis who behaved in bizarre ways, seeing and interacting with a world very different from the one that we experience. Profound personal growth can occur in the first stage of yoga, purifying ahankara, while still supporting our day-to-day lives.

The ancients saw all of life as an energy flow and they wanted to *be* the energy phenomenon. Their practices did not support functioning in society. Modern yogis can use pranayama to move closer to the idea of the self as an energy phenomenon, without going all the way there.

Figure 2. Formation of ahankara and the two stages of yoga

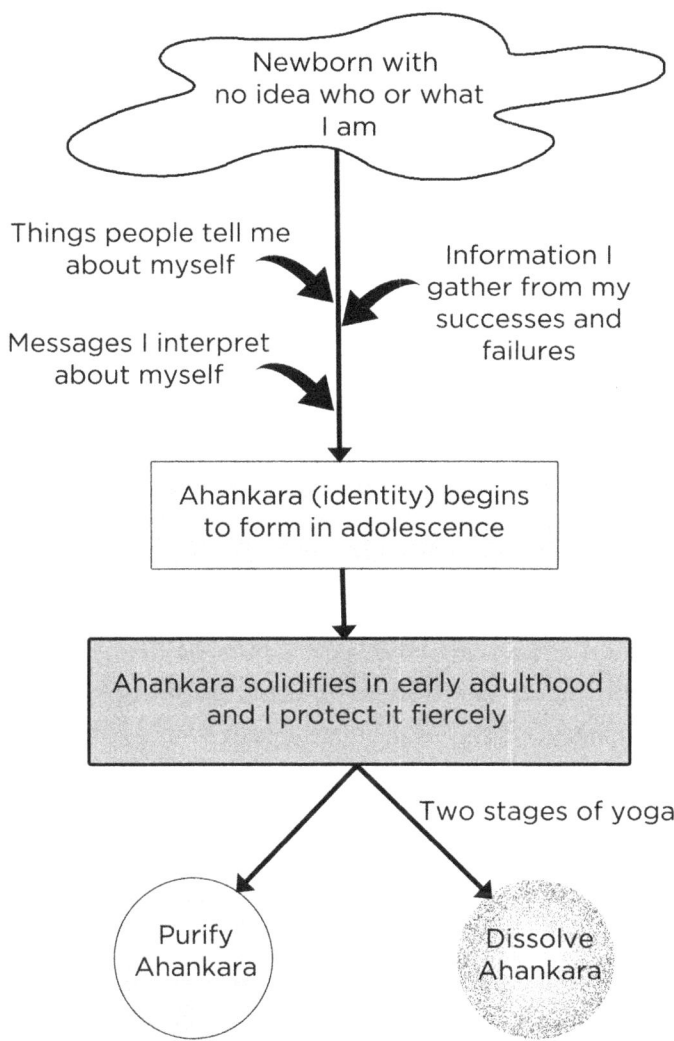

Ahankara and Patanjali's Classical Yoga Philosophy

Nearly two thousand years ago, Patanjali systematized the school of yoga now referred to as classical yoga. He wrote the *Yoga Sutras* and described the eight limbs of yoga. Because his doctrine continues to influence yoga practice and philosophy today, we will look at the way his philosophy ties neatly into the concepts of ahankara.

Patanjali describes five causes of all suffering, known as the *kleshas*, or the afflictions. **The first klesha is *avidya*, usually translated as ignorance of what we really are.** Avidya is the state of having no ahankara. This is the newborn baby who has no idea who or what it is. A person might taste of avidya in a situation where he does not fit in, such as starting a new job or visiting a foreign country. Having no sense of self is a very insecure state. That is the state of avidya.

The second affliction arises because we need an identity. We create a self-sense, just as the bird builds a nest. **Patanjali calls this self-concept *asmita*.** Asmita and ahankara are both terms referring to one's identity, but arising out of different traditions.

We then encounter the afflictions of attraction and aversion, Patanjali's third and fourth kleshas: *raga* and *dvesha*. If something reinforces the ahankara, it attracts us (raga). If something threatens the ahankara, we avoid it (dvesha). Think about your friends. You choose companions who reinforce your ahankara. You avoid people who challenge your ahankara, unless, for example, it's part of your ahankara that you do not deserve safety and that you should constantly be challenged. Then, you might pick friends that support confrontation and self-destruction. Overall, though, the mind works to protect the ahankara.

Once our identities are solid, we feel content. We like our ahankaras. **Then the fifth affliction, abinavesha, arises. This usually translates as "fear of death"**: *I am afraid of the whole thing falling apart, so I work extremely hard to maintain it. I won't let anything shake my identity. It contains some falsities and flaws, but I don't care. I have no place else to stand, so I hold onto it.*

We cling to ahankara like that drowning man in the river who builds a raft to survive. He becomes so overwhelmed with attachment to his raft that he remains oblivious to the waterfall threatening to destroy him up ahead. That raft is ahankara. Someday, our ahankaras are going to fall apart. When we die, ahankara dissolves. That is why death is so painful. We must leave everything and everyone behind. Still, we cling to ahankara like the drowning man on his raft, even though the waterfall surges just around the bend.

Figure 3. Ahankara and Patanjali's kleshas, or five afflictions

Patanjali's Affliction	Relationship to Ahankara
Avidya	The state of having no ahankara. *Born into the world, I have no idea who I am.*
Asmita	The equivalent of ahankara. *I develop a self-sense.*
Raga	Attracting that which enforces ahankara. *I cling to that which validates my sense of self.*
Dvesha	Repelling that which challenges ahankara. *I push away that which threatens me.*
Abinavesha	Fear of ahankara falling apart. *I fear death, so I cling to my identity tenaciously.*

Modifications of Ahankara

Throughout our lives, we modify our ahankaras whenever we identify something as part of ourselves. We link ourselves to objects, views, and people so that they become fibers of our beings. For instance, I say, "I am a teacher." Being a teacher becomes part of my ahankara, and my students become the proof. I feel proud of the students who reveal my success as a teacher *(raga)*, and I distance myself from students who do not resonate with my teachings *(dvesha)*. My peers bear witness to my credibility as a teacher. Over years of struggle, I feel more like a teacher and less like anything else, and I cling to my job tenaciously *(abinavesha)*.

Meanwhile, I see someone driving a nice car and I say. "If I had a car like that, I'd look as good as he does." I work hard to buy a new car, and the car becomes part of my ahankara. I drive by an incredible house on the mountain, and tell myself that, if I could have that house, I would feel so important. I do whatever it takes to acquire that house, and the house becomes part of my ahankara. So I take a job, a car, and a house and modify them to make them parts of me.

I look out and see a fascinating world, and I do not leave it there. I possess it. That is *my* land! That is *my* career! That is *my* enemy! I make the whole world about *me*. **My life becomes all about bolstering my ahankara and pushing away all that threatens my ahankara. Each time I do this, my ahankara is reshaped.**

The Urge to Merge: How Energy Works

Being human can sometimes feel like treading water—barely keeping our heads above the surface while mighty currents threaten to pull us under. Mortgages, family responsibilities, and careers are just a few of the forces in our lives that create stress and wear us down. Pause for a moment to ask yourself how many times in the last week you have felt afraid, lonely, or insecure.

According to yogic philosophy, we have two opposite drives within us that respond to this unstable condition of the soul. The first drive tells us to "keep it together" at all costs. Do whatever you need to do to function in the world, protect yourself, and maintain your separate existence.

The "keep it together" drive starts as soon as the soul forms and becomes self-aware. Some of the old texts describe the soul as emerging from *Brahman.* Brahman was a timeless, formless state of pure consciousness. **Think of Brahman as an ocean of consciousness and the soul as a drop that splashes up from that ocean.** The drop spins around, sees the ocean, and cries "Wow!" As soon as it reacts in this way, the drop asks, "Who said 'Wow'?" Next the drop realizes, "Oh, I said 'Wow.' Who am I?" This question—this differentiation from the whole, from the ocean—generates a great deal of insecurity *(avidya)*.

The drop, or soul, is now self-aware and fears annihilation. If it falls back into Brahman, it will dissolve back into undifferentiated consciousness and cease to exist as a separate entity—the equivalent of dying. **The soul wants to feel like its own entity, to feel real.** So we create a stressful career because the challenge validates our existence. We earn degrees and certificates, generate wealth and have children, all because our soul drives us to separate from Brahman.

But, in our individuality, it can feel like the whole universe is against us. Proving our separate existence and protecting ourselves from Brahman can be exhausting—and when we lose any of the elements that support our identity—the job, the wealth, the relationship that make us "real"—we feel like our world is falling apart.

When we grow weary, yoga philosophy teaches, our soul remembers what it was like to be a part of Brahman, having no cares or concerns. That's when the second drive kicks in, and we feel a desire to dissolve into something larger than ourselves.

This second drive is the "urge to merge." It further divides into two opposing pulls: *prana* **and** *apana*. Prana manifests as an urge to merge with spirit or soul; it is energy streaming inward and upward. Apana appears as an urge to merge with nature and the external world; it pulls downward and outward. When we follow either prana or apana, separation vanishes, and we experience bliss.

> *"Just as a bird on a leash is pulled back to its place, so also the soul is held back by prana and apana. Thus prana attracts apana in the upward direction, and apana attracts prana downwards. "*
> *—Swami Kripalu*

To understand apana, look at cows grazing in a pasture. They meander through a field and chew grass. In complete oneness with the earth, they pass on their genes, eat food, and eventually return to the earth. Instead of agonizing over career moves and cholesterol levels, imagine thinking "I'll just follow the cow in front of me."

As humans, we experience apana when our attention flows to people and things outside of us. We taste the sweetness of apana when we dance, engage in a rich conversation, view a stunning landscape, or make love to another human being. In the act of lovemaking, individuality dissolves and each being becomes the primal man or the primal woman, coming together to share their genes. We find freedom in this oneness with nature, this connection with our animal selves.

In the other direction, prana invites us to go deeply within ourselves, leave the world behind, and merge with spirit. It aches to return to the center. Imagine yourself with absolutely no external awareness. Your attention could only go inside. That is prana. It flows into the soul.

Experiences of prana are less concrete than encounters with apana, but they make up with their sweetness what they lack in frequency and tangibility. When prana is stronger than apana, we feel introverted and reflective. The outer world seems vague, and the inner world lights up. An especially deep meditation epitomizes a powerful experience of prana. As we leave a yoga class, feeling blissfully radiant, the lights outside seem more beautiful and bright because of the heightened light inside you. Such inner radiance provides a strong experience of prana that indicates a brush with spirit.

Figure 4. Distinguishing the two pranas

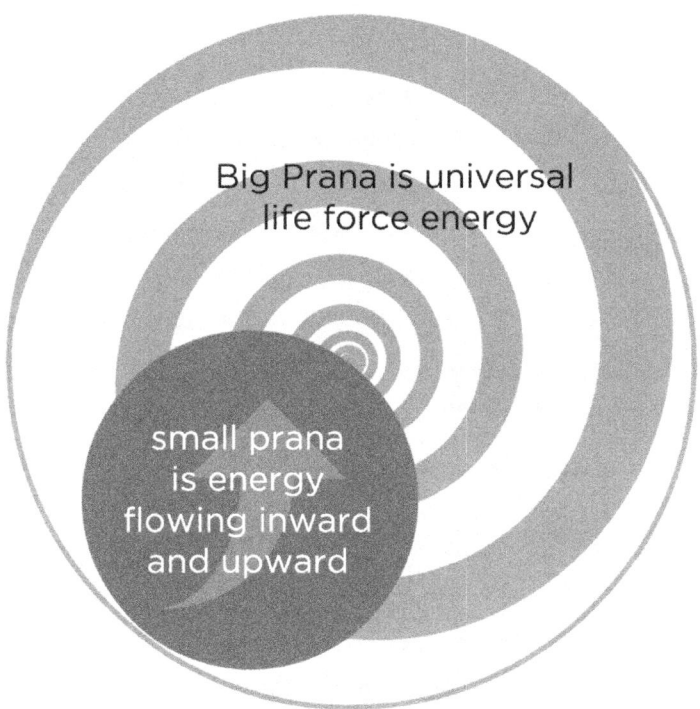

The prana pulling inward and upward is not to be confused with the universal life force Prana. The terms are the same in the yogic texts, but the smaller prana, energy flowing in a specific direction, is only part of the larger Prana, the source of all life.

Here the two pranas are distinguished by a lowercase "p" (prana) for the inward, upward force and an uppercase "P" for universal life force energy.

Figure 5. Prana and apana flow in opposite directions

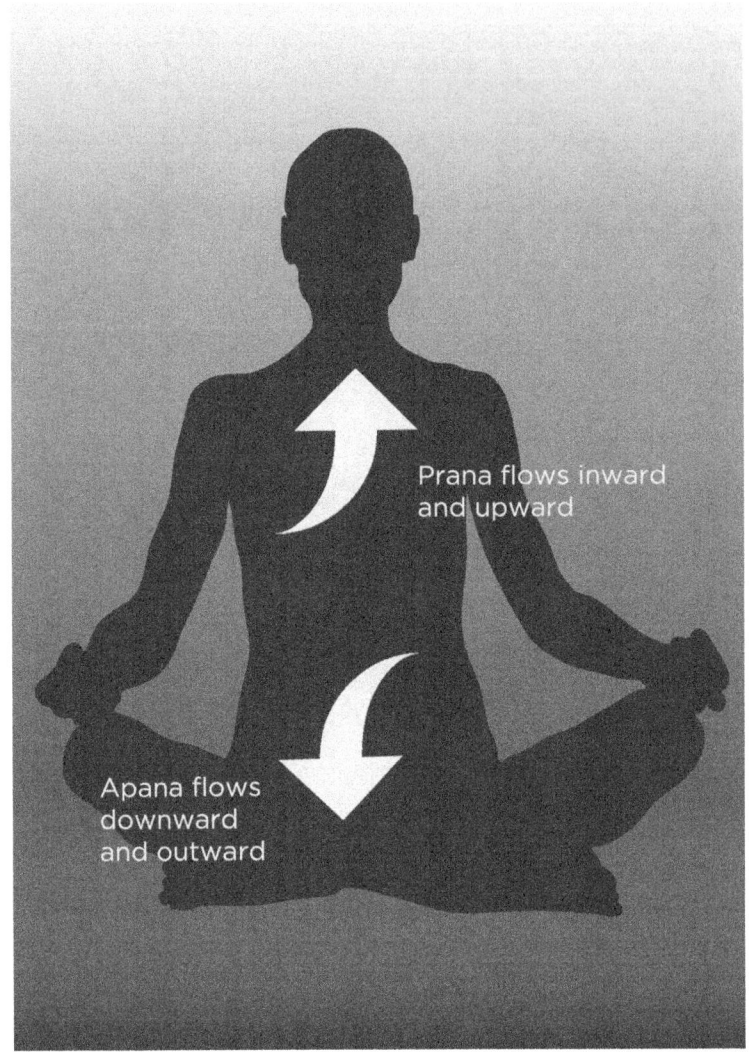

In the process of merging with something larger than ourselves, prana or apana can grow to be strong enough to make ahankara uncomfortable. When this happens, ahankara feels threatened and works to stabilize the energy. It does this through countless built-in safety mechanisms that we use to automatically adjust our energies without even thinking about it. Among our trusty energy dumps are the box of cookies near the water cooler at work, the Starbucks at the end of the block, and the hours of web surfing. If our energy threatens ahankara in the least bit, we reach for one of our tools to raise or lower it back to a comfortable level.

Yoganand

During a time when I was looking closely at prana and apana in my life, I attended a family reunion. About 40 of us stood in a room with a television blaring in one corner and a huge food table against the wall.

A conversation sparked between two of my uncles when one of them asked the other, "How's your daughter doing?"

"She's fine," the other uncle answered, nodding politely. Then he casually gestured to the food table. "I'm gonna get some food."

The topic of religion arose in a circle of aunts and cousins. After only a few words, everyone sensed discomfort, and one person turned to the television. A moment later, everyone else followed suit. They tuned into a football game for five minutes, then came back to discuss a brand new topic.

My family had set up the entire reunion so a person could quickly escape anytime he felt triggered. Admittedly, relatives are the most capable people in the world to trigger a person. It was Ram Dass who said, if you think you are enlightened, visit your family.

We set up our lives so that, anytime we are triggered, there is an easy way out.

Look around your car, and you will probably find a dozen escapes, or energy levelers: a phone to make calls or listen to music, a snack in the glove compartment, a magazine in the back seat. **We surround ourselves with distractions so that we can keep our ahankaras stable.** Because we need them to function rationally in society, having our ahankaras shaken in the external world is extremely scary. But this is why so little personal growth happens. Ahankara needs to be shaken in order for a person to heal and evolve.

The ancient yogis were not afraid to disturb ahankara. They worked hard to strengthen prana and weaken apana. **You could even say that a goal of yoga is to make prana stronger and apana weaker, to disconnect from the outside world and the stimuli that go with it.** The ancients welcomed experiences of controlled disturbance, because they knew those moments would lead to greater experiences of spirit and grace. To support this work, the ancient yogis built their lives around spiritual practices, especially pranayama. They often removed themselves from society and lived in secluded dwellings, such as caves. There, it did not matter if their ahankaras fell apart. For today's yoga practitioners, who live in society, it takes more effort to create safe environments to do deeper spiritual work. Still, it can be done.

In the shelter of my meditation room, I can let go of my worldly roles and the armor that I carry all day long. Everywhere else I have to hold myself together. In my own sacred space, I go to the vulnerable place where my ahankara can soften to a state in which it can be purified.

Thus, we contemporary practitioners can take from our ancestors the goal of increasing prana and decreasing apana, even if in much smaller doses than our predecessors.

Figure 6. Prana and apana are two opposing drives to merge with something larger than ourselves

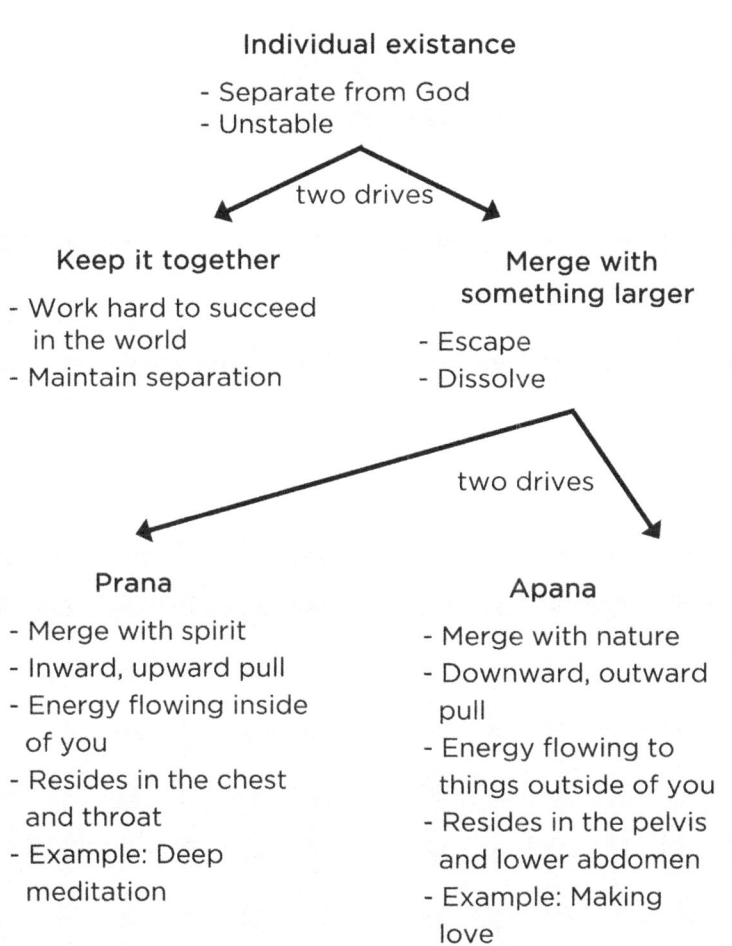

The Battle of Liberation

When the inward, upward pull of prana grows strong enough, it tries to completely dissolve the ahankara into oneness with creation. Because of the ahankara's attachment to apana, which pulls downward and outward, this attempt to merge with spirit inevitably fails. According to the *Hatha Yoga Pradipika*, prana resides in the chest and throat. Apana lives in the pelvis and lower abdomen. As prana intensifies and ascends, it eventually reaches a point where it turns back down, dives into the body, and attacks apana.

Prana and apana begin to battle, and **apana breaks out its three big heroes: anger, fear, and sexual energy.** Take a moment to think about these three energies in your life. They can easily overwhelm us, and when they do, we react in ways that further bind us to the world.

Look at fear, for starters. If I fear that I am unsafe, then I want a better apartment, more insurance, or a safer car. All of those things cost more money, so I work harder to obtain them, thereby rooting myself more deeply in worldly matters that are outside of me.

Anger becomes a driving stream of energy that reaches out toward someone else, creating thoughts and emotions, and trying to create actions. If you insult me at a party, I bind myself to you through anger. There might be 20 other people in the room, but they disappear, and I want to destroy you. The angrier you make me, the more real that drive becomes.

Sexual energy compels us to have children or seek a partner. I bind myself to another, no longer a "me," but part of a "we." Through these cycles, I become more enmeshed in the external world, fulfilling apana's desire that I merge with nature.

Apana uses these three intense energies to warn the soul of the danger of losing everything in the outside world if it follows prana inward. Apana holds up the yogi's shame, fear, attraction, and low self-esteem, and warns the soul, "If you merge with spirit, you'll lose your money! You'll lose relationships! You'll lose your power!" Prana responds with the rationale, "What I get from those, I can get from spirit." Apana needs to be convinced, so the battle continues.

The only way that prana can win is if the yogi sits back and simply watches the fight, without choosing sides. Prana then engulfs apana and transforms all the energy into pure prana. That energy flows up the yogi's spine to the crown of her head. Her ahankara evaporates, and she merges with spirit. **According to the yogic model, she is enlightened. She is liberated.**

The moment the yogi interjects her judgments into the fight, no longer an objective spectator, apana wins. If, for example, the battle stirs up sexual desire and shame, the yogi might allow this thought to consume her: "I am a disgusting person." With this judgment, objectivity vanishes, and apana prevails. The yogi can return to fight the battle time and time again, delving deeper each time, but **the secret weapon is total objectivity.** Can the yogi sit back, see her whole self, and allow prana and apana to churn her body?

The churning, called *chalana* in Sanskrit, reveals ugliness, baggage, shame, guilt, and fear, all of which can be excruciating to observe, especially without judging oneself. The churning also reveals the yogi's magnificence, brilliance, and pure potential, qualities that can be equally challenging to accept as facets of the self. Apana loves when the yogi feels undeserving. The yogi thinks," I can't be that magnificent. Somebody will shoot me down." Apana smiles.

In order to sit back and see who he really is, the yogi must expand. With his greatness, vulnerability, ugliness, and splendor laid before him, the yogi is challenged to accept himself as the whole blend. Finding it hard to be so complex, he tries to simplify. He might tell himself "Overall, I am a good person." But if he truly looks at his intricacies, he would say, "I am a magnificent and wonderful person, and I am a lustful person. I am an angry person, and I am a greedy person. I am a very compassionate person. I am the most loving person you'll ever meet, but if I get angry, I am an absolute beast!"

Something inside of us goes on tilt when we open up to take in all of who we are. We need a way to see and integrate all of this experience, and we also need a way to contain it. That is where pranayama comes in. **Practicing pranayama strengthens prana and the ability to hold complex experiences.** The stronger prana grows, the more it dives down into apana, stirs us, and brings to light all that we need to see in order to return to a state of pure soul.

A number of tantric texts, including the *Bhagavad Gita* (a chapter within the *Mahabharata*) and *Ramayana*, allegorize this battle within the yogi. In one myth, the gods and the demons have been fighting for years. The gods pray to Vishnu and ask how they can defeat the demons, and Vishnu tells them to go churn the ocean of milk. When they try to do so, the gods realize it is impossible to do this by themselves. Their only option is to enlist the help of the demons. Together, the gods and the demons churn the ocean and watch the nectar of immortality rise to the surface. The demons grab it first; then the gods snatch it and run away.

This myth represents the battle of prana and apana within the yogi. The gods seeking help from the demons represents prana going down to merge with apana. The churning is the practice of pranayama. The nectar of immortality is the yogi's truth rising to the surface to be seen and integrated. The gods absconding with the nectar is prana ascending with all the energy and converting it into pure spirit.

Is Apana the Enemy?

The ancient texts paint apana as a villain, but **apana is neither good nor bad.** If someone's prana is especially strong, he is an introvert. If a person's apana is strong, she is an extrovert. Apana is limited, since it only cares that we pass on our genes, live "normal" lives, and die. But even that approach can hold a sweetness that we encounter as humans.

Yoganand

I witnessed the beauty of apana once when I was visiting my family in South Carolina. I walked into the living room one evening and saw my mother rocking my sister's newborn baby. When I saw the expression on my mother's face, all I could think was, "She is in bliss."

Apana can give us bliss, but apana wants us to think that bliss is all we ever need. It wants us to be satisfied with that bliss. Prana essentially says that bliss is wonderful, *and there's more.* Usually, the blissful experiences offered by prana and apana conflict, and a person can have only one or the other at any given time.

I love my family, friends and my career, all of which connect me to the world and are expressions of my apana. If I sit down to meditate, and I follow the pull of prana into the depths of my soul, there comes a point where I have to let go of my worldly connections, even my family. If I worry about whether they will be there when I come back, I cannot go deeply into my meditation. If I can temporarily cut those links, I can delve deeply. Then, I must let go of the depth to come back to my worldly life. When I do, I can appreciate those people and my environment even more.

Apana, as it is classically perceived, wants the yogi to be attached only to the earth and nature. It is not bad, but it is not everything. It is part of a whole that wants you to think it is everything.

By the same token, **prana is not everything either.** If the yogi finds herself following the upward pull of prana, she can only go so far before getting stuck. She must be willing to go back down. **Just as the gods could not churn the ocean of milk without the help of the demons, prana cannot free the yogi's spirit without apana.**

Although the image offered in many ancient texts is a battle between prana and apana, some yogis feel uncomfortable with violent metaphors. One can also think of the two energies in proportion to each other. There is always a ratio of prana (energy flowing inward) to apana (energy flowing outward). As apana gets stronger, prana gets weaker. As prana gets stronger, apana gets weaker.

Vice into Virtue

Although apana's strongest weapons—anger, fear, and sex drive—can easily consume us, the ancient yogis created an effective technique to deal with them. This technique involved **disarming the intense emotions by removing their labels** so, instead of being anger, fear, or sexual desire, these imposing emotions became pure energy. For example, if anger arose within a yogi, it was apana. If he disarmed it, removing the label of "anger," it became pure prana.

> Ancient yogis worked to disarm intense emotions, so the energy behind the emotions could become pure energy.

How does one disarm emotions? If someone insults me, it produces a surge of burning energy that I would typically experience as anger. If I stay with the anger, the energy streams outward, attaching me to my aggressor. **If, instead, I close my eyes, turn inward, and let go of my offender and the situation that upset me, what remains is not anger, but a powerful surge of pure energy.** That energy can feel like ecstasy, even though it originated as anger.

The challenge is that it is extremely difficult to "let go of my offender," or to remove the label of anger or fear. When I feel angry after being insulted, I clearly believe what my enemy said, or I would not have reacted to it. The same is true with fear. I would not become afraid of a situation unless I believed there was something to fear.

Furthermore, how easy or difficult it is to disarm emotions depends heavily on one's conditioning. Someone conditioned to associate shame with sexual energy finds it difficult to sit with sexual feelings and allow them to be neutral energy. For a person who feels inferior, insecure, or vulnerable, it is a struggle to watch fear arise. Anger presents difficulty for someone whose ahankara feels easily threatened.

The angry or fearful reaction is not always rational. Consider the person who is terrified to touch a snake that he knows is harmless. Our will melts when we are placed before strong anger or paralyzing fear, especially if the anger or fear is pre-rational or irrational. **Our strongest fears are our oldest fears, those that formed before our rational minds developed.** Also incredibly powerful are present-day fears that make us feel as helpless as when we were small children.

In the *Bhagavad Gita*, the brave and seasoned warrior Arjuna begs to be released from the situation that reveals his deepest helplessness—the breakdown of his ego structure. Because Arjuna is a yogi, he has the wherewithal to turn to his teacher when emotions overwhelm him and say:

> *My heart is overcome by weakness, and my mind is confused. I request You to tell me, decisively, what is better for me. I am Your disciple. Teach me who has taken refuge in You.* (Chapter 2, Verse 7)

Even this valiant warrior struggles with overpowering feelings.

While it is very difficult to take an emotion, remove its label, and see it as simply energy, a yogi cultivates the skill by doing postures and pranayama in ways that strengthen prana. The strong prana partially dissolves ahankara, and, with the softened ahankara, charged experiences from the past are released from the unconscious and rise up to be seen. **The yogi practices witnessing that which arises in each moment. Strengthening this witness within the context of one's yoga practice makes it easier to observe charged experiences objectively in the other areas of your life.**

About two thousand years ago, there was a yoga tradition in India called the *Pashupata Marga*. *Pashu* means "animal," *pata* means "to descend." The Pashupatas saw apana as a binding energy, binding us the way a farm animal might be bound. In India, water buffalo are abundant, and they have rings in their noses. When a person rides a buffalo, he puts a belt through the ring and sits on its back. The animal turns in whichever direction the rider pulls the belt. **We are like those water buffalo, pulled by the rope of apana in the form of emotions, desires, and fears.**

Pashupata yogis worshipped a Hindu god named Rudra, the god of fear. When their practices produced fear or other "animal emotions," they did not push them away. A Pashupata yogi would never say, "I fell deep into a meditation this morning, then anger arose and spoiled the whole thing!" If anger, fear, or sexual energy appeared in their meditations, the Pashupatas smiled, because they possessed the technique of reframing the energies and converting them into pure prana. To them, this practice of disarming was the key to liberation.

In the *Bhagavad Gita*, Arjuna's teacher instructs him to do his duty, the practices that raise energy. He is then told to fight the battle without attachment. This text uses the term *yajna*, literally meaning "sacrifice." We are told that all actions bind the soul or strengthen our ego identity, except those that are performed as yajna. **Yajna is an offering to** the soul or an action performed to free the soul from ego identity.

> *Human beings are bound by action other than those done as Yajna (sacrifice). Therefore, O Arjuna, do your duty efficiently as a service to Me, free from attachment to the fruits of work.* (Chapter 3, Verse 9)

Thus, "reframing" emotion is the skill that the yogis worked to hone. It is the path of converting vice into virtue, or the path of integrating the whole self. This process makes our anger, fear, and sexual energy divine and essential. These energies need to be reclaimed because they are fuel. If we converted all of our anger, fear, and sexual drive into pure prana, it would dissolve our ahankaras and take us straight to God.

Prana and Apana in Your Life

You're working at your desk, when suddenly a voice inside you says, "I'm hungry." That urge is Prana. We rarely ever question that urge. Similarly, suppose you are lying on your couch watching TV, and a voice says, "Your arm is falling asleep. Roll over." That voice is Prana. You respond without thinking about it. **We rarely experience prana and apana directly. Instead we experience them as faint urges.**

Quite often, as Prana rises up within us, it becomes feeling or sensation. That sensation turns into emotion. Emotion leads to thought, and thought leads to action.

Consider this example: Jennifer is in a meeting, where her boss asks her a challenging question and she has an urge to leave the room. She feels danger. That feeling becomes the emotion of fear. She has a thought that she'll say she has to go to the bathroom, and she goes. Figure 7 shows this pattern, offering one way in which urge, or Prana, evolves into action.

In a different progression, a thought might generate an emotion. If Nick is planning to go out on his bike and thinks about getting hit by a car, that thought might lead to the emotion of fear, which could influence his action, and he'll decide he doesn't want to go out on his bike. These stages can loop together in numerous ways, but most of our actions can be traced back to prana and apana.

The practice of pranayama can help us tune in more clearly to the messages from our Prana. Because pranayama intensifies the Prana, it magnifies inner experience. This means we suddenly feel the anger, the need to be okay, or the fear that previously lingered beneath the surface. The entire process in Figure 7 becomes magnified, allowing us to understand the flow of prana and apana. If fear drives many of our actions throughout the day, the heightened Prana will show us the fear. If we can see the fear, we can see what we do because of the fear. Then, we can take responsibility for it. The stronger the Prana, the more magnified the initial urges become. **If our Prana grows strong enough, that which hides from our everyday consciousness comes into clear view.**

Figure 7: One model for how Prana works

Model	Example
Prana/urge ↓	*Jennifer's boss asks a challenging question and she has an urge to flee*
Feeling/sensation ↓	*Because of her urge to escape, she senses danger*
Emotion ↓	*Her feeling of danger becomes the emotion of fear*
Thought ↓	*Fear causes her to think of saying she has to go to the bathroom*
Action	*She excuses herself and goes to the bathroom*

Strengthening the Container

A fundamental goal of yoga is to see one's whole self, but we must first prepare for this work. Many of us sit on intense issues that could blow us out of the water if they came rushing to the surface. For this reason, **traditional yoga work involved building a container, or a witness, strong enough to hold charged experiences that rise to the surface to be seen and integrated.**

The "container" is a metaphor for ahankara. It includes every structure that we identify as ourselves: our minds, bodies, and belief systems. **Ahankara translates literally into "what I believe myself to be."** It can be closely aligned with what we really are, or completely different from what we really are. If what I believe I am is far from the truth, the distance will result in tremendous distortion and pain. If I think I am strong but am not, I might commit to doing more than I can actually do. If I think I know more or less than I actually know, that incongruity will create conflict.

From a yogic perspective, most of the pain in our society comes from people not knowing what they truly need or want. Challenging the container provides a reality check, and yoga offers **two key ways to challenge one's container. The first is by holding postures past the point where our ahankara says we can hold them.** Historically, yogis risked small physical injuries to find out the truth of how strong they were. **We are not encouraging you to injure yourself!** Often, however, we can hold a posture much longer than we think we can (again, *without* injuring ourselves). When we do, we open to new understandings about our strength, power, and potential.

The second way in which yoga can challenge one's container is by raising energy through asana and pranayama. The increased energy generates emotion, so this practice allows us to see how much we are capable of feeling.

We have already seen how ahankara resists change. Ahankara also resists having its flaws exposed. A person experiences this friction in daily life when he sees something about himself that he doesn't like and pushes it away. Sometimes, when confronted with a truth, we deny that truth and hold onto the old way of seeing ourselves. Other times, there is a moment, conscious or not, where we let go, accept the truth, and move forward.

When this process is intentionally generated through yoga practice, it is called *tapas*. Tapas literally means "friction," "the heat," or "fire that friction can cause." Some say that in order to break a habit, a person must resist it seven times. Whether or not that is true, it illustrates the concept of tapas. To hold onto a truth until all resistance fades and it becomes natural is tapas, and it purifies ahankara.

In addition to giving us two key ways to challenge the container, yoga provides two other important benefits that help strengthen one's sense of self. The first is **increased sensitivity.** Because yoga heightens our sensitivity, a yogi may be so aware of himself in daily life that he grows and learns from his day-to-day experiences. Secondly, **yoga induces expanded states** that reveal aspects of ourselves that we either do not see fully or do not see at all in daily life.

Another image used to illustrate this process of integrating our truths is captured by the Sanskrit word chalana, which we mentioned briefly earlier in this chapter.

Chalana means "to churn." Just as milk is churned or agitated, causing the butter that was in the milk all along to emerge, so our true nature emerges when ahankara is churned. Again, this churning can come from daily life experiences, holding yoga postures, or raising energy through asana or pranayama.

The vehicle for transformation when our containers are challenged is the conscious choice to fully *experience* **the charged situation rather than** *endure* **it.** We all have tasks, people, or events to which we close down as soon as we near them. We tighten up and endure, repeating the old patterns rather than practicing tapas, staying open, and inviting the new.

> Four ways to strengthen the container with yoga practice:
> 1) Holding postures to challenge ahankara
> 2) Raising energy to challenge ahankara
> 3) Increasing sensitivity to see truths more clearly
> 4) Inducing expanded states to reveal otherwise hidden aspects of ahankara

Remember our caveman from Chapter 1? He interpreted two different situations as threats and clamped down to both, first to the saber tooth tiger and second to his angry wife. Escaping the tiger required him to shut down in order to survive. Other circumstances similarly require an appropriate level of endurance. A child of abusive parents needs and loves his caretakers, even though they cause him fear and pain. Feeling the full degree of this conflict could make it impossible for the child's ahankara to develop. He needs to partially close down in order to survive.

However, this shutting down can quickly become a habit. The caveman did not *need* to shut down to his wife in order to survive. Rather, he developed the habit of shutting down early on and carried that coping mechanism into his marriage.

Without even knowing it, we make endurance a way of life, and we learn to put up with almost anything. For instance, if Bob finds himself in a traffic jam, his true feelings might be frustration and helplessness because he needs to get somewhere and is unable to move. Rather than allowing himself to feel powerless and vulnerable, he shuts down. He turns on music, makes a phone call, and tells himself it will be over soon. While this might seem like a positive coping mechanism, it still involves Bob denying his initial emotions and acting from a desire to avoid those emotions, rather than acknowledging and accepting them.

Yoganand

Many times, we endure yoga classes. If I lead students into a posture and have them hold for five minutes, most folks drop into enduring mode. They tune out or channel their energy into angry thoughts at me. Their bodies strengthen, but no mental or emotional transformation occurs. When they release the posture, a wave of relief washes over them and they mistake that relief for the bliss of yoga.

The same thing happens with pranayama. Pranayama raises energy, which the mind wants to discharge, so it creates distractions. Thoughts might arise, such as, "Maybe I should clean the house" or "I want to go for a walk." Those thoughts are the mind's smoke screens, created to conceal the intensity of the moment.

On the opposite end of the spectrum from enduring, we have the choice to fully experience the realm of sensations, thoughts, and emotions in a given situation. Instead of tuning out during a yoga posture, a student who practices staying present while part of him screams *"I'm going to die!"* experiences the situation completely and strengthens his container. If the yogi raises his energy through pranayama, and watches thoughts and feelings come and go, he practices containing the energy and strengthens his sense of self. Every time a person has a stressful meeting at work and thinks, "I don't know if I can do this," and she does it with awareness, feeling the stress without getting lost in it, she strengthens her container. Whenever we fully experience something that holds a charge for us, we strengthen our containers and open ourselves to the possibility of transformation.

When we endure life, we lose the joy. We lose the sweetness and the connection with spirit. We tighten up. We cannot shut down to the pain without shutting down to the pleasure. The beauty in the world invites us to experience. The fullness of life invites us to experience. Even the pain invites us to experience, because that pain can be a catharsis and a release, moving us closer to the reality of life. Human existence spans from blissful to agonizing, but we tone it down to "sort of okay" and "not too bad"—a far cry from blissful and agonizing.

When we experience a situation, we open. **To endure life consumes energy, and every time we shift from** enduring to experiencing something, the energy that held it in a distant place is released, and it enlivens us.

Yoga practice, especially deeper yoga practice, invites us to experience fully, but **we have to choose to feel.** No technique is strong enough to force it to happen. This does not mean we need to visualize or create the experience. It means we make a conscious choice to open to it.

Sometimes, in the process of strengthening the container, we find that we must pause to mend cracks. For example, Joe was a devout yoga practitioner who grew up with an abusive father. As an adult, he needed to stop to heal his container from the abuse in his childhood. He realized this one holiday when he was planning a visit with his family, and he felt paralyzed at the thought of being with his father. When he looked closely at his reaction, he saw that he had grown so in touch with himself through his yoga practice that he felt intense rage toward his father. His yoga practice had reconnected him with feelings he had pushed away for most of his life. Now those emotions lurked so close to the surface that Joe feared the intensity of his own anger.

Joe dropped back into endurance mode to get through the visit with his family, and, after the trip, he realized that his ability to contain his experience was so weak that if all of the anger toward this man came to the surface, it would blow him apart. Blowing apart might mean he would melt down, scream, or collapse. He might even attack his father. Part of him would fragment because he could not handle the extreme emotions.

Joe turned to his yoga to work with his lingering feelings. He practiced staying aware during challenging pranayama and asana sessions. He wrote in his journal to integrate thoughts and emotions. Those practices strengthened Joe's container enough to allow the stuff to come up, and the container became a crucible. It held the reaction and allowed integration to occur.

Joe's container became strong enough that he could eventually be with his father and feel his emotions without crumbling. Memories still arose and the enraged little boy inside screamed, "That S.O.B.!" at the man who beat his mother and never talked to Joe. At the same time, the adult knew that the past could not change, and that his feelings had nothing to do with the man sitting across the table from him now. In the past, he had hurt Joe, but he was a different person today.

The little boy still felt the extreme emotions, and if adult Joe said to the little boy, "You should not feel that way, because your father did the best he could," that would only divide him. So Joe's adult voice responded, "Yup. He was an S.O.B. alright!" and he smiled, because he knew he could feel all of his anger and contain it. Somehow or other, as Joe let that little boy feel what he needed to feel, he integrated.

Yoganand

Once you patch cracks in your container, you can choose to turn back to strengthening it. A lot of folks focus so heavily on healing that they sometimes neglect what lies beyond. Once you heal, keep working to grow.

Swami Kripalu pursued liberation with everything he had, and I followed his model. He told his disciples to burn with ardor. Yoga was not made for sick people. Sick people can benefit from yoga, but Yoga was created by skinny little men living in caves who wanted to be enlightened by blowing their ahankaras out of the water. Maybe they all should have settled down with wives and families instead, but they felt there was another way. They worked to enliven their whole bodies, dissolve their ahankaras, and experience oneness with all of creation.

Vishvamitra and Sukadeva

Swami Kripalu tied together two separate myths from the *Mahabarata* to illustrate the difference between a strong container and a weak one. The first is the tale of a yogi named Vishvamitra. In Hindu mythology, Indra rules the first of seven heavens. Whenever a yogi raises energy through intense tapas, Indra's throne starts to shake. If the yogi continues raising energy, Indra bounces off his throne and the yogi takes his place as the new king of heaven.

Vishvamitra meditated for a thousand years and held his breath for so long that smoke began to pour out of his ears. As Indra's throne started to tremble, he looked down and said, "Vishvamitra is shaking the whole universe! He's going to throw me off my throne!" Acting quickly, Indra called on Mina, the most beautiful of all the celestial maidens, and told her, "Go down and dance for Vishvamitra."

Vishvamitra was sitting stoically with laser beam concentration, when suddenly he heard tinkling bells. He opened his eyes to see Mina standing before him wearing tinkling bells and nothing else!

Next thing Vishvamitra knew, years had passed, and he was chopping wood behind his house. Mina drove by in their Subaru, taking the kids to soccer practice. Vishvamitra said, "Wait a minute! How did I get here?" And he realized Indra had deceived him. So he set up a trust fund, kissed his family goodbye, and headed off into the woods to find another cave and start his yoga discipline all over again.

In the myth of Vishvamitra, Indra symbolizes

ahankara, the ruler of the yogi's universe. Indra shrewdly manipulated Vishvamitra, just like the ahankara weasels to protect itself when it feels threatened by the yogi's intense practice. Vishvamitra's container, too weak to withstand Indra's temptation, crumbled. **When a yogi practices at an intensity beyond the strength of his container, he too will collapse.** He might not drink for 25 years, and then, all of a sudden, while he's meditating he can taste the martini in his mouth. He tells himself, "Maybe I could have one drink again. I can handle it. I'm a yogi now." Indra smiles, and the yogi does not have a clue. Suddenly that yogi is Vishvamitra chopping wood in the back yard, asking, "How did I get here?"

The other story Swami Kripalu used to illustrate the difference between a strong and weak container is that of a yogi named Sukadeva. Sukadeva's yoga practice generated a charge of Prana so potent that a hole popped open in the top of his head and his soul shot up like a tongue of fire into the sky. On the way to Brahman, or universal oneness, a soul must travel through seven heavens. In the first layer of heaven are beings called *gandharvas*, people not yet liberated but with too much good karma to exist on earth. In heaven, they can eat, drink, smoke, and have all the sex they want with no repercussions. Possessing no physical bodies, gandharvas basically play for a lifetime until they have used up enough good karma to be born on the earth to work again.

As Sukadeva's soul flew through the sky toward Brahman, he was seen by a group of gandharva maidens frolicking in a stream. The nymphs looked up at Sukadeva and said, "What a beautiful man! Sukadeva, come play with us!" Sukadeva heard their voices, looked down at the beautiful maidens, and kept going.

The difference between Sukadeva and Vishvamitra is that Sukadeva held it together where Vishvamitra fell apart. Our challenge is to work toward the level of Sukadeva, which means looking closely at desires when they arise. **When a temptation shows up, it might be ahankara distracting us to avoid becoming unstable, or a sign that we need to look at an issue that has not been fully integrated.** Maybe twenty years have passed, and a drink, a pill, a needle, an ex-boyfriend—you name it—arises into the yogi's awareness. She must look at it and ask herself what is really going on.

If her container is strong, she can see the desire for what it is, and she does not need to fear it. She does not need to squash it either. Sukadeva did not yell at the maidens to go away and leave him alone. If he had done that, he probably would have popped right back into his body and started all over again. He saw them, and he felt no charge.

When the difficult stuff comes up, it is an opportunity to do what we could not do before. Maybe I find that whenever I begin to succeed at something, my inadequacy appears and I stop. If I notice the pattern objectively and keep following the success, I will expand. **This practice gives us a chance to heal and a chance to grow into another level of freedom.**

The Merging of the Sun and Moon

So far, to understand how yoga and pranayama work, we've looked at the model of prana, apana, and ahankara. We've also examined how Patanjali's classical yoga philosophy ties into the concept of ahankara.

We'll now turn to another traditional model for understanding *pranayama* that is frequently referenced in the ancient texts – the model of the sun and moon merging within the yogi. We'll examine this model by itself, and we'll also look at how it fits into the other philosophies we've discussed so far.

Consider the phrase hatha yoga. The word hatha combines sun (ha) and moon (tha). The word yoga means union. So hatha yoga translates into sun-moon union, the coming together of the sun and moon.

The sun is situated in the pelvis and lower abdomen, and represents the passions and drives of the flesh: anger, fear, lust, and desire. The ancients found these energies to be relentless, driving us and burning us like fire. Most of us have burned at some point with desire, fear, lust, or anger. The sun is the same as apana.

The moon is in the head, representing the rational self (ahankara). The moon is controlled and regular—calm, cool, and serene. It moves in a precise circle and astronomers can predict its location and phase for centuries into the future.

The sun (apana) and moon (ahankara) are connected by a closed channel called *sushumna*. If sushumna opened within a novice yogi, the sun and moon would unite, and the yogi would cease to exist. **If, however, the yogi could first develop a strong enough container or witness, he or she could withdraw into that witness as sushumna opened, and experience that he or she is not the body nor mind but rather free spirit, timeless and eternal.**

So, Hatha Yoga connects the passionate animal self with the cool, rational self. This is similar to the model in which prana goes down and fights with apana, and then the two of them ascend as one energy. In both models, the passionate animal self merges with the rational self. The rational self has to dive down into the animal self and see it for what it is. The animal self will then lose its charge, its resistance, and its attraction, so it can just be, without the rational self trying to make it something else. (This can be interpreted as total self-acceptance.) Then the two energies can rise up as one. **Hatha yoga recognizes that we need both the animal self and the rational self to become fully alive. We need the sun and moon to unite. We need prana and apana to ascend as one energy.**

Here is a verse from the Hatha Yoga Pradipika about the sun-moon model:

> *The sun and the moon regulate time in the form of day and night. The sushumna nadi eats time. I have told you a most profound secret.* (Chapter 3, Verse 17)

Again, the sun is apana, or the animal self, and the moon is ahankara, or the rational self. The phrase that "the sushumna nadi eats time" means that the yogi feels blissfully eternal when sushumna, the channel connecting the sun and moon, is open.

Another verse from the Hatha Yoga Pradipika describes the sun-moon paradigm:

> *A yogi with his half-closed eyes fixed on the tip of his nose and his chitta* (mind) *well balanced and perfectly composed, gradually absorbs the moon and the sun. He attains that completely perfect supreme place, completely refulgent, illustrious, that is the primordial seed of all. What more can be said?* (Chapter 4, verse 41)

This verse refers to the sun and moon uniting, so there is no longer a division within the yogi. It goes on to describe the effects of this merging, which are ultimate peace, transcendence, and liberation.

When humans are born, the moon (rational self, or ahankara) is less developed than the sun (primal self, or apana). Drives rule, and the rational self is pulled along for the ride. To the sun, one's needs and desires are supreme. It does not matter whether he deserves what he wants, whether it's available or at what cost. If a young child's needs are not met, the sun burns with all its power. Over the course of time, the moon grows, with encouragement from one's parents, and begins to temper the sun. A child learns that he sometimes does not get what he wants. He learns to postpone gratification, to get what he needs and desires without creating more pain for himself. He learns to manage conflicting needs and to compromise.

As humans continue to grow, assuming we are healthy, the moon grows stronger in its ability to control the sun. We become more rational, and we like the stability that the rational self brings. For many people, the sun becomes an enemy that threatens their happiness and cannot be trusted. A conflict forms between one's security and freedom, between creativity and safety, between staying as we are and continuing to grow.

To open sushumna is to bring the sun and moon together. Within the safety of a yoga practice, the sun can flow unrestrained because it is contained. We have no need to direct it outward. At the same time, the moon becomes latent by withdrawing into the witness. Eventually, that infusion of energy from the sun completely dissolves the yogi's ego, mind, ahankara, or witness into pure consciousness, also known as *buddhi*. **The yogi then feels freedom as pure as the wind in the trees and power as pure as that of the burning sun.** Some traditions call this experience of such profound energy "the vision of god." This vision is described in the following passage from the Bhagavad Gita:

> *Lord Krishna, the great Lord of yoga, revealed His supreme majestic form to Arjuna. Arjuna saw the Universal Form of the Lord with many mouths and*

eyes, and many visions of marvel, with numerous divine ornaments, and holding divine weapons. Wearing divine garlands and apparel, anointed with celestial perfumes and ointments, full of all wonders, the limitless God with faces on all sides. If the splendor of thousands of suns were to blaze forth all at once in the sky, even that would not resemble the splendor of that exalted being. (Chapter 11, verses 9-12)

The moon, of course, resists the sun's unleashing. For sushumna to open would be a temporary death to a part of us that is successful. It would be the end of the ahankara we've worked so hard to build. Think of all the gifts we receive by being stable, calm, and rational. The moon perceives that it has much to lose and much to fear when sun energy rages. Aren't all spiritual practices threatening to the ego? Spiritual practices take us to another realm; they aren't rational, so the ego mind doesn't know what to do with them.

The texts encourage us to move slowly, gradually exposing the ego mind to more and more energy, rather than moving too quickly and causing damage. The texts also teach us to strengthen our witness so we do not become afraid. In so doing, we will eventually come to the place where there is no one for the sun energy to drive, because the witness or ego has dissolved back into pure consciousness, or buddhi.

This verse from the Hatha Yoga Pradipika speaks of the need to move gradually when doing this work:

Just as lions (anger), elephants (fear) and tigers (lust) are gradually brought under control, similarly Prana when well restrained and regulated is gradually mastered. Otherwise it harms the sadhaka. (Chapter 2, verse 15)

We will learn more about doing this work at a reasonable pace in the next section, "The Path of Self-Responsibility."

Figure 8. The merging of the sun and moon within the yogi

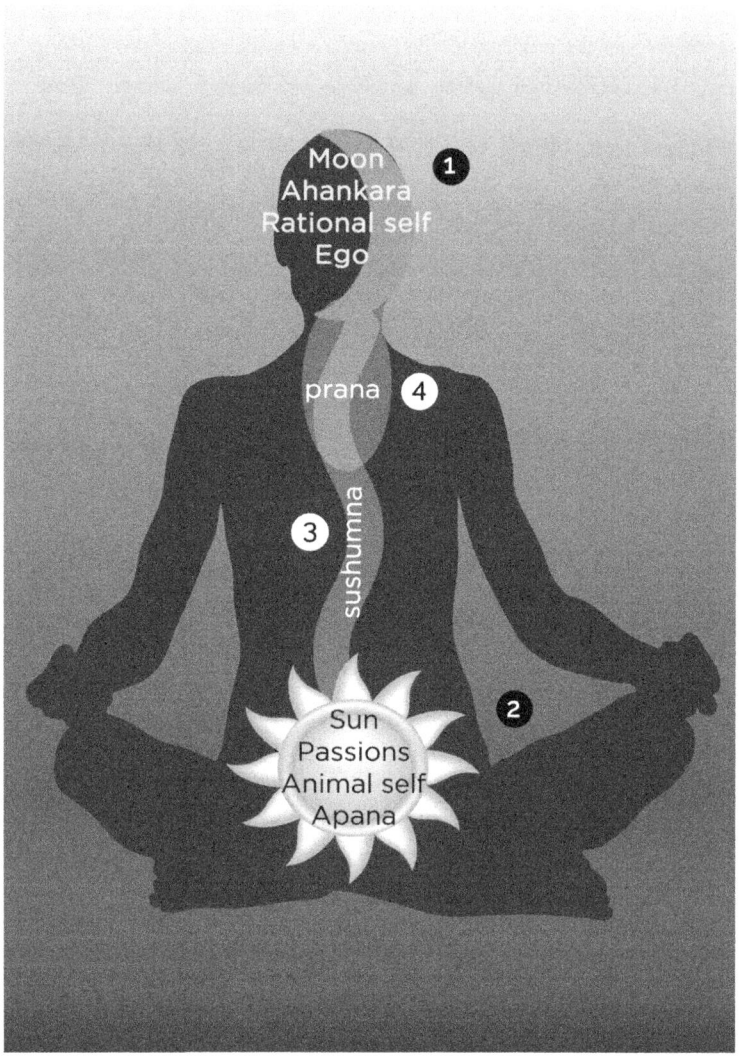

1. The moon is the rational self that lives in the crown of the head. It fears the sun and wants to contain it or build a wall between itself and the sun. The moon is the same as ahankara, or asmita, our sense of self.

2. The sun is the passionate, animal self that lives in the pelvis and lower abdomen. It is the same as apana. It wants to burn wildly and freely. Its most powerful forms are anger, fear and sexual energy. It is strongest when we are first born and have not yet been conditioned. At that time, we are primal beings of raw energy and impulse.

3. Sushumna is the central nadi (channel) that connects the sun and the moon. It is closed for the average person, as the moon builds a wall between itself and the sun, between reason and passion. Traditional yoga practices open this channel, and, when it is fully opened, the sun and moon unite. The yogi feels both pure freedom and ultimate power, unrestrained prana, or "yoga fire." The yogi is liberated.

4. Prana is an inward, upward pull, a desire to merge with spirit. When prana is strong enough, it tries to dissolve ahankara, but ahankara is attached to apana. So prana has to attack apana. Prana wins when the yogi's witness is strong enough to watch the battle objectively. Prana transforms all the energy to pure prana or "yoga fire." Sushumna opens, the sun and moon unite, and the yogi is liberated.

The Path of Self-Responsibility

"The power of Prana that is increased through pranayama, breathing exercises, is the speed of an airplane. But everyone cannot digest that speed. So it is better that one grows slowly and steadily." —Swami Kripalu

As a yogi works with his energy through pranayama, it's essential that he remain connected to the ways in which changing his energy affects every aspect of his experiences. This helps ensure that his pranayama will lead to healing and enlivening, without causing any harm.

Yoganand

I had just turned 30 and had been diving head first into my sadhana since I was 18. Over the past 12 years, I had gradually increased my pranayama practice from one to five hours a day, and found myself at a point where I craved both progress and external validation to prove my dedication to my yogic path.

I met with my teacher to talk about a frightening experience in my practice. During our discussion, my mentor validated my experience, offered some guidance, and extended his blessing to increase my pranayama by one hour each day.

I was beside myself with excitement. I felt thrilled for the opportunity to go deeper into my sadhana and grateful for the blessing and trust from my teacher and father figure. I felt a little scared, but my fear was eclipsed by my ecstasy.

I proceeded with care. The past 12 years had shown me that increasing my pranayama more than 20 minutes at a time left me emotional for two or three days. Now I was increasing by three times that amount.

The next day, I called a staff meeting with the ashram bookkeeping and purchasing departments that I supervised. I told them I was going to increase my pranayama and would be a basket case for a couple of weeks. I asked for their help and understanding: "If I look at you like a deer in headlights, please tell me it's okay. If I snap at you, challenge me, because it is not me; it's my disturbed energy."

I arose at 3:20 the following morning to begin my new regimen: one and a half hours of pranayama to start the day, followed by my postures, then another hour and a half of pranayama. Two more 90-minute pranayama sessions at lunch time and the evening for a total of six hours of pranayama per day.

Sure enough, the next two weeks found me a mess. I walked into work feeling like everyone was staring at me. My insides tightened, and I was afraid someone would ask me to deal with something I couldn't handle. I was in no place to reach out and help my staff, even though I was their manager. As I watched them begin to bypass me, my paranoia multiplied.

The days passed, and I began to adjust to the heightened energy generated by the additional hour of pranayama. After a couple of weeks, I once again became more rational. My fears waned. My system stabilized. I could perform my job effectively again and life returned to normal once I had acclimated to the heightened state of energy.

That is how it works when you live in an ashram. Most modern yoga practitioners cannot go to their bosses and tell them things will be a bit crazy for a week because they are increasing their pranayama practices. Erratic practice shocks our systems. **When we live in the world and**

have external responsibilities, we must adjust our pranayama responsibly. If you practice 30 minutes a day, your system adjusts to 30 minutes a day and that becomes the norm. If you allow three days to pass without pranayama and then do an hour on the fourth day, that will create a jolting shock to the system. A person could practice three hours a day on a regular basis with less disturbance than practicing one hour a day three times a week.

Yoganand

Feeling highly emotional, as I did after increasing my pranayama, is a typical result of raising more energy than one can deal with. For me, paranoia flip-flopped with anger.

Another manifestation of immoderate energy is the sudden reemergence of old desires and behavior patterns. Imagine a yogi sitting on his cushion, sinking into his pranayama practice, when, out of nowhere, comes a thought of a woman he dated five years ago. "I wonder if she's still around. I should give her a call." Where did that come from? He hasn't seen her in five years! Similarly, people come back after practicing a lot of pranayama and say, "I haven't smoked marijuana in 20 years, but suddenly I'm craving a joint." **The thirst for an old habit is the mind looking to dump heightened energy and asking what worked in the past.**

Is it good or bad that pranayama can bring up old desires and difficulties? **If a person can integrate it, it becomes a doorway to clarity.** An alcohol problem from the past might resurface during intensive pranayama. Maybe the person has moved beyond it, but part of her still fears that she will relapse. What if she became strong enough to look at that old desire, say, "Nothing there for me now," and walk away fearless? **That is what it means to overcome a fear.**

If the threat is valid, stay away. A person who sees a rattlesnake in her path should go in the other direction. Many of our fears, however, grow out of imagined threats. If a person comes upon a rope in the road and frantically screams, "There's a huge snake over there! Don't go that way!," that is when it's valuable to go back and say, "That's not a snake. It's a rope."

The rope signifies the ways in which, quite often, we fear too quickly. In asana practice, we feel something in our bodies, jump to the conclusion that it's pain, and turn away from the experience. If we stop and look, what we think is pain is usually mere sensation, just as the snake is a harmless rope. Moreover, that sensation can lead to tremendous self-knowledge. It can take us to places of truth, showing us where we hold fears and revealing the defenses that arise when our ahankara (moon or rational self) feels threatened.

Aliveness in certain parts of our bodies scares us. At some point in our lives, many of us were either hurt in part of our bodies, or used our bodies to hurt someone else—whether our fists from physical aggression, genitals from sexual abuse, or jaws from yelling—and we fear that it might happen again. When the pranayama sends energy to that part of the body, it presents an opportunity to look more closely. Maybe we are different people now. The situation might have shifted such that we can let go of the fear that holds us less than fully alive.

When it helps us to examine and transcend a desire or fear, the excess energy is beneficial. We harvest the Prana, consume it, and it nourishes us. But we only reap these benefits if we are able to integrate the heightened energy. If a yogi cannot integrate it, he should focus less on pranayama and more on strengthening his container.

Yoganand

In the old days of the ashram, yogis were led to activate an exorbitant amount of energy. At the time, the focus was on the grace and letting go of the surrender practice done by Swami Kripalu. The belief was that giving ourselves to the energy would heal and lead us to the highest. It might have, but not before taking us through the valley of the shadow of death.

Many people came to the ashram and plunged into these practices, without first building strong containers. Their energy invaded their sense of self, and traumas from the past rendered them dysfunctional. Victims of their own energy, they spent days sitting in their beds, staring out of windows. With their most haunting demons reawakened and tormenting them, they simply could not operate. After some time, our teacher realized that he needed to shift the focus from surrender to willful practice, and teach his students to strengthen their containers.

This illustrates the need for keen discernment and a strong capacity to hold heightened energy. **Without sharp discrimination, it is extremely easy to build enough energy that the container starts to shake, and the energy automatically discharges.** Many people create routines in which they generate energy, spend energy; generate energy, spend energy. Entire yoga studios function around this model of building energy only to dump it. Sincerely dedicated practitioners gather at the studio for a challenging practice. When class ends, they feel open, powerful, and uninhibited, so they all go out to a bar. They establish cycles in which they balance their energies just right, flirting, eating, or using intoxicants enough to have a good time, but not so much that they cannot wake up for yoga the next morning. Rather than partying all night long or not at all, they figure, "I can party until midnight, and still get up on time." That is venting the energy, bleeding it off, or draining it away.

In Swami Kripalu's tradition, the yogis worked with a different model. They wanted to raise energy and stabilize; raise energy and stabilize.

Yoganand

People who had never before been in his presence would spontaneously cry when Swami Kripalu walked into the room, because he kindled an inner glow that radiated outwardly and was tangible to others. We could feel his sadhana. I think, from his perspective, he lived in a different universe from us. The reason? Every time a yogi raises his energy, his perception changes. Needs and desires shift. The whole world looks different.

For years I worked with the volunteers at Kripalu. I would tell them this: Pick a day when your energy feels particularly low—self-esteem in short supply and feeling down. That day, go into the dining room and make a list of all the people to whom you feel attracted. Then, pick a day when your energy soars. Confident and needing nothing, walk through the Dining Hall and note those who interest you. The list will be different.

Energy influences all of our choices: the people we marry, the colleges we attend, the careers we pursue, how happy we are, how much money we make, and where we live. **When our energy is low, the world is harder; when**

our energy is high, the world is easier. If our energy gets too high, we become afraid and unstable. The yogis wanted to raise the energy to a point where it was a little bit unstable, and stay there until that level of vitality normalized.

Swami Kripalu was a renunciate. The volunteers at Kripalu lived in an ashram. How should modern-day yoga practitioners living in the world practice? **We must learn to watch our energies, focusing on how much pranayama we are doing overall, while also stepping back to observe the effect of each pranayama technique on our energies.** We should stop before the point of automatic discharge, when we find ourselves drinking, smoking, or overeating to subdue the intensity. Instead, we should raise our energy about 60 to 70 percent toward the point where we feel the need to dump the energy, and practice being there. Even at 60 or 70 percent, the desire to vent the energy comes. When we cultivate a level of energy that generates a desire to dump, *but we don't discharge it,* we strengthen the container.

On a basic level, this path is one of self-responsibility. It requires sincere practice and asks us to look closely at ourselves, deciding what would most support us on all levels. When we do, we build tremendous discernment and learn to relate to our energies in ways that heal, enliven, liberate, and move us closer to whole.

Fully alive

Yoganand

In fifth and sixth grades, I got into a lot of fights with kids on the playground. The principal told my parents he would suspend me if it happened one more time. I never got into another fight, but I squelched part of myself to achieve this restraint.

How many times, as children, do we hear the message that we are too vital and alive? Too inappropriate? That we need to control ourselves? Then we grow up and begin seeking approval from other adults. Soon we control ourselves as much as they do. We do everything to fit in. While we might be successful in society's eyes, we lose something in the process.

Yoganand once met a horse that epitomized this trade-off.

Yoganand

My wife and I were staying at an estate in Costa Rica, where we were leading a workshop. One afternoon, the owner of the estate offered us a horseback trip through the rain forest. Now I would rather walk beside a horse than sit on its back, but my wife enjoyed riding, so I went along. They put me on a gentle horse whose Spanish name translated to "Bartender," and all Bartender could do was walk behind the horse in front of him. Showing no initiative whatsoever, he was happy to mosey along, make a loop around the property, and return to his feeding place. With my horseback riding challenges, Bartender and I got along just fine.

We had ambled through the rain forest and emerged into a big field when, all of a sudden, I heard a thunderous rumble and looked up. The owner of the estate and his wife rode toward us on big black stallions with long manes. It seemed impossible for them to have all four feet on the ground at the same time. In fact, when the owner tried to stop, he could not. His stallion had to walk in a circle. That horse had so much vitality it could not stand still.

I looked at the stallion and I looked at Bartender. I realized that Bartender had lost something along the way. He was half alive, which was enough to get from the food trough to the water bowl to the barn. Bartender fit in, and he did not have to deal with all the problems that a stallion has to deal with. Bartender had it made, and he probably felt as if his simple, easy life was worth what he had given up to achieve comfort and simplicity. But when I looked at the stallion, I could see he was fully alive.

Most of us, somewhere along the way, chose the path of Bartender over that of the stallion. As Bartender, we fit in and we are okay. As Bartender, we are lovable. That is wonderful, but now that we have mastered the skill of being Bartender, what would happen if we went back and learned to be the stallion again?

Yoganand

I rode Bartender just fine, but if I had mounted that stallion, he would have thrown me off in an instant. To ride the stallion, I would have to cultivate some skills. That might mean *practicing, taking lessons, building strength, poise, and balance. In time, I could ride that stallion.*

In the same way, **we can use yoga to tap into our animal energies and learn to live more fully alive**. Living fully alive is 10 magnitudes greater than having a good day. When the ancient texts refer to the idea of being fully alive, it is the feeling a person has 10 seconds before an orgasm. Imagine walking around in such a state all day long! The sunrise looks utterly amazing. Standing in line at the grocery store feels blissful. Everybody else might think you're crazy, but you don't care, because you are fully alive. *You are fully yourself.*

To move in the direction of living fully alive, the primary skill to cultivate is self-knowledge, because we have a lot of energy to protect. We cannot forget the valuable lessons we learned as Bartender. This means respecting every environment we enter. We would not want to bring that stallion into a china shop. We have responsibilities not only to ourselves, but also to the world. **The challenge lies in finding balance—accessing the stallion energy while remaining respectful and interactive with our surroundings.** We have to channel the energy in ways that support our growth without hurting others. The stallion might feel like going out on the town and chasing mares, but, if I am the one riding that stallion, I have to say, "No, you're going to exercise and go back to the barn."

> To live more fully alive, the primary skill to cultivate is self-knowledge.

It requires enormous responsibility to manage that kind of energy, but the possibility stands right before us. To access it, **all we have to do is stop saying no to greater levels of aliveness.** A fountain of energy flows abundantly within us, and we have dug ditches so that it drains away. Classical yoga practice teaches us ways to stop the energy drain and strengthen our containers. Once we learn to do this, the energy will rise automatically.

Ultimately, this path boils down to energy. All of the techniques—postures, pranayama, meditation—work to activate and channel energy. The bigger the charge behind the practices, the more powerful and absorbing they become. One could say, then, that yogis are sculptors of energy, with the yoga techniques serving as skillful hands, the energy acting as malleable clay, and spiritual riches and radiance emerging as masterpieces.

PART II

PREPARATIONS FOR PRANAYAMA

CHAPTER THREE
IDEAL CONDITIONS FOR PRANAYAMA

The ancient yogis felt that it was imperative to practice pranayama with the appropriate conditions. **Everything had to be just right for the practices to be most effective.** These conditions are outlined in the several hatha yoga texts written between the 12th and 17th centuries; the *Gheranda Samhita* and the *Hatha Yoga Pradipika* give the most thorough and grounded treatment of pranayama. **While we may not adhere to the ancient instructions literally, their general messages can help guide our contemporary yoga practices.**

The *Gheranda Samhita* states:

> *Four things are necessary for practicing pranayama. First, a good place. Second, a suitable time. Third, moderate food. And lastly, purification of the Nadis.*
> (*Gheranda Samhita*, Chapter 5, Verse 2)

We will look at each of these conditions here.

A Good Place

> *The practice of Yoga should not be attempted in a far-off country, nor in a forest, nor in a capital city, nor in the midst of a crowd. If one does so, he loses success.* (*Gheranda Samhita*, Chapter 5, Verse 3)

Performing a practice like pranayama helps to connect us with raw, unfiltered feelings. Because of this, a safe environment is essential. Stepping back from the literal translation of the verse, let's look at how the intention of each point supports safety.

Why not practice pranayama "in a far-off country"?

Yoganand

Visiting India, I remember walking through a town, unable to read signs or understand the people. I needed to find a restroom, but had no idea how to ask. I entered a store where cans and bottles labeled in Hindi stocked the shelves. I could have been standing in a hardware store, a drug store, or a grocery store, for all I knew. I felt incredibly insecure. Such an unfamiliar environment lacks the safety required to look inside and see one's raw truth. Instead, it is a place to clamp down and get one's needs met.

Similarly, practicing pranayama "in a forest" was dangerous to the yogis writing these ancient texts. They had to worry about being attacked by tigers and snakes. While we might not have ferocious animals lurking in the shadows, the text cautions against making ourselves vulnerable in any precarious environment.

The suggestion to avoid pranayama "in a capital city" indicates that excessive activity hinders the process. The authors are essentially saying, "Practice in an environment where you can relax and will not be disturbed by an intense flow of activity."

Being "in the midst of a crowd" can feel threatening and evoke vigilance. A situation in which you are surrounded by strangers and feel that you have to watch your back does not support the practice of pranayama. Practicing intentionally in a group, where safety is established, is much more fruitful.

> *In a good country whose king is just, where food is easily and abundantly procurable, where there are no disturbances, let one erect a small hut, and around it, let him raise walls.* (*Gheranda Samhita*, Chapter 5, Verse 5)

"A good country whose king is just" again refers to stability. Conditions such as war or famine continually pull inhabitants into survival mode, and do not allow for the secure environment required to go inside and do deep emotional work.

Building a small hut with walls alludes to the privacy required to dive into deeper yogic practices and remain open to whatever those practices elicit.

> *And in the center of the enclosure, let him dig a well or sink a tank. Let the hut be neither very high nor very low, let it be free from insects. It should be completely plastered over with cow dung. In a hut thus built and situated in*

> *such a hidden place, let him practice pranayama.*
> (*Gheranda Samhita,* Chapter 5, Verses 6-7)

The enclosure described above provides privacy; the well or tank provides the yogi with a water source, so he doesn't have to go to the community well in the village to obtain water. Practicing pranayama with flies or mosquitoes landing on the skin is miserable and distracting, which is why the enclosure needs to be free of insects. In India, cow dung and urine are used to clean, because they have antiseptic properties and keep diseases down. Sanitation, therefore, is the reason for the cow dung.

Overall, the teachings for creating "a good place" encourage the optimal situation, which boils down to a safe, relaxed space. However, while the authors speak entirely of external factors, internal conditions are even more important. **When we devote heart and mind to the practice, we can ultimately practice pranayama anywhere.**

A Suitable Time

> *The practice of yoga should be commenced by a beginner in spring or autumn. By doing so he obtains success and he does not become liable to diseases.* (*Gheranda Samhita,* Chapter 5, Verse 9)

Pranayama creates a churning in the body, which helps the practitioner sense what is happening on deep levels. Because this churning can generate physical heat, practicing pranayama in summer temperatures that hover above 100 degrees, as they do in India, becomes unpleasant. In the winter, dry air in both North America and India can cause mucous membranes to partially dry up. A beginner would therefore want to avoid a lot of vigorous breathing in either the summer or winter months, and instead begin the practice in spring or fall. Once the practitioner is more familiar with the techniques, he or she can continue the practice into summer or winter.

Does that mean starting pranayama in the middle of summer or winter is disastrous? No. **To benefit most from the ancient teachings, one must take them lightly and consider *why* they make the recommendations they make.** The ancient gurus wanted to make it as easy as possible for practitioners. They knew that, when the process becomes difficult, we tend to tighten up, jump into survival mode, and plow blindly through using brute force. This contradicts the essence of yoga, which is to move closer to self-understanding. **By creating comfort and ease around the practice, we are more apt to build awareness and cultivate self-knowledge, moving in the direction of wholeness.**

Moderate Food

He who practices Yoga without moderation of diet incurs various diseases and obtains no success. (*Gheranda Samhita*, Chapter 5, Verse 16)

If you have ever practiced yoga with a full belly, you probably did it only once. Besides creating immense discomfort, overeating consumes excessive energy and dulls the internal experience. This undermines the primary purpose for practicing pranayama—to increase energy and heighten internal sensitivity so our inner truth can be revealed.

> *Pure, sweet, and cooling foods should be eaten to fill half the stomach. Eating these sweet juices with pleasure and leaving half the stomach empty is called moderation in diet.* (Gheranda Samhita, Chapter 5, Verse 21)

This verse has generated much debate about what constitutes "pure, sweet, and cooling." Ayurvedic medicine sheds some light on the question by recommending certain foods as cooling or heating, but it is unclear what is meant by pure or sweet. Does sweet refer to granulated sugar? Honey? An apple? Likewise, what constitutes pure? These questions remain elusive. **What's important is that the text essentially encourages nourishing food that the system digests easily.**

> *Half the stomach should be filled with food, one quarter with water, and one quarter should be kept empty for practicing pranayama.* (Gheranda Samhita, Chapter 5, Verse 22)

Having personally adhered to these guidelines for two and a half years, I strongly discourage them. Following the text literally means the stomach never completely fills up. If the stomach never fills, it begins to shrink. As the stomach shrinks, filling it half full means eating even less. In the depths of my practice, I stood five feet, 10 inches tall, and weighed 108 pounds. Although I took it too far, I learned a valuable lesson about following the texts too literally.

For the contemporary practitioner, sticking to the teachings word for word is not as important as capturing their essence. **Here, the text basically says, "Practice** moderation in diet." Eat in a way that does not weigh down the system or inhibit breathing.

One reason for restricting the diet is that **formal pranayama creates a specific energy pattern in the body,** which wears off with time. For this reason, the *Hatha Yoga Pradipika* says to practice pranayama three times a day: morning, noon, and evening. Other texts add a fourth session at midnight. By doing this, the yogi receives another infusion of pranayama when the energy pattern starts to wear off. **With regular practice, he can then live in that energy pattern.** When it comes to diet, maintaining this energy pattern requires the yogi to eat enough to satisfy his needs, but not so much that it interferes with the practice. Ancient yogis worked to control the diet so that it was steady.

How do these principles apply to the modern-day practitioner? To benefit most and maintain a deep practice, **do your pranayama on an empty stomach.**

> *A yogi should avoid harsh, sinful, or putrid food. Or very stale food, as well as very cooling, or very much exciting food.* (*Gheranda Samhita*, Chapter 5, Verse 30)

This verse basically discourages foods that shock the system. Ice cream, for example qualifies as "very cooling." Caffeine is considered "exciting." **Ultimately, pay attention to your body and learn what disturbs your system.**

> *He should avoid early morning baths, fasting, or anything that gives pain to the body. It is also prohibited for him to only eat once a day or to not eat at all. Though he may remain without food for three hours.* (*Gheranda Samhita*, Chapter 5, Verse 31)

Yoganand

I spent some time living in India, where the tradition dictates that ordinary people bathe every morning, but yogis do not. Being considered a lay person, I was told to bathe early in the morning in unheated water and outdoor temperatures of 50 or 60 degrees. For groggy, less refined bodies, the shock of a cold bath can kick-start the system in the morning. For yogis coming out of meditation with heightened sensitivity, jumping into a cold bath creates an unpleasant shock to the system that distresses the body.

The second half of the verse basically re-emphasizes the concept of not filling the stomach with food, but rather maintaining a steady supply of nutrients to avoid extreme hunger, to free the breath, and to promote balance.

Regulating his life in this way, let him or her practice pranayama. In the beginning, before commencing it, he or she should take a little milk and ghee daily. And take his food twice daily, once at noon and once in the evening. (*Gheranda Samhita*, Chapter 5, Verse 32)

In one of his books, Swami Kripalu wrote that Anuloma Viloma, a foundational pranayama, stimulates the colon. When the colon is stimulated, it works more powerfully. The colon serves two functions: moving waste products through the body and preparing them for elimination, and removing water from fecal matter. Practicing too much pranayama or increasing the amount of practice too fast can cause the colon to work so well that it malfunctions. It can take the water out of the excrement to the point that it becomes impacted and leads to constipation.

In his book *Play of Consciousness*, Swami Muktananda describes how his excrement came out scorched, because of practicing excessive pranayama. The fat content in whole milk or ghee (clarified butter) is recommended to lubricate the system, keep things moving, and prevent constipation.

Purification of the Nadis

The fourth condition for practicing pranayama is purifying the *nadis*. **A nadi is a channel or tube through which something flows;** the root, "nad," means "to flow." Some yoga texts teach that the nadis are energy channels that exist only in the subtle body. Others say they exist in both the physical body and the subtle body. **Here, we are working with the premise that anything subtle has a physical counterpart, so nadis reside in both the physical and energy bodies.** *Nada* is that which flows through the channel. For our purposes, *nada* is the flow of life force energy, undiluted by rational thought.

> A nadi is a channel or tube through which something flows.

On a physical level, our bodies are nothing but tubes. Consider the circulatory system. Veins, arteries, and capillaries transport blood through our bodies. The lymphatic system parallels the circulatory system with its elaborate network of vessels transporting protein-containing lymph fluid throughout the body. Moving on to the nervous system, electro-chemical impulses travel through nerves, making them nadis as well. The digestive system is essentially one big tube, averaging 30 feet long from one end to the other. If you've ever seen a picture of the lungs, you know that they are big tubes branching into little tubes into even smaller tubes, ending in alveoli, small sacs that hold air and are surrounded by capillaries—tubes wrapped around tubes. Even our cells have tubes. Physically, we are a huge network of tubes, or nadis.

If the tubes become blocked, what happens? Imagine wrapping a tourniquet around your arm and squeezing it tightly. Your circulation would reduce, which is another way of saying the nadis would close, and your arm would become numb. When the colon gets blocked, we call it constipation. How well do you feel when you're constipated? **Whenever nadis become blocked, there is an increase in numbness and a corresponding decrease in aliveness.**

Yoganand

I once had a big mopey Maine Coon cat named Zackary, who mostly lazed at the foot of the bed or on his favorite windowsill. Every now and then, Zackary acted out of character and tore around the house like a lightening bolt. I began to notice that these frenzies occurred just after Zackary had sprung out of the litter box with a kick. It was obvious with Zackary when the tubes were open and when they were blocked.

What causes our tubes to tighten? Tension, for one. Since muscles are basically tubular cells inside of tubular connective tissue, tightness in the muscular system is a blockage of nadis. Lack of exercise is a second cause of blocked tubes. Inactivity decreases circulation and leads to stagnation of interstitial fluid, causing toxins to build up. Tubes can also become blocked through injuries. The most obvious example is a paralysis, where a nerve is cut and the body loses its ability to move. Swelling, tearing, immobility, scar tissue, and other aspects of injuries similarly block tubes in the body's systems.

Sometimes, we *choose* to block our tubes.

Yoganand

Years ago, in my role as a volunteer counselor at Kripalu, I worked with a woman who believed she was always 15 pounds overweight. She told me, "I have tried everything to lose weight. Nothing works. I want to try yoga and self-discovery techniques to manage my weight." We worked on conscious eating and found support for her within the community, and she lost 10 pounds. Then, one day, she came into my office terrified, saying, "I know now why I'm always 15 pounds overweight. When I'm thinner, I look better. Men give me more attention. I'm afraid I'm going to get hurt, like I did in the past."

Somewhere along the way, a protective inner mechanism told this woman, "You've got too much vitality. You are going to get hurt." As a result, she subconsciously chose to carry 15 extra pounds, which slashed her vitality, made her feel less attractive, and decreased the stimulation she received from others' attention. Once she became aware of this cycle, shedding the pounds and keeping

Our nadis become blocked through:

- Tension
- Lack of exercise
- Injury
- Choice

them off meant she needed to find a level of aliveness with which she could comfortably exist. It also meant facing the fact that she had previously chosen to reduce her vitality. It required discrimination and a strong enough container to hold the vitality and make it work for her, not against her.

When we feel more than we are comfortable feeling, our minds often diminish our experience. One way the mind does this is by tightening the body. When it tightens, the body becomes rigid. Whether from muscular tension, immobility, injury, or choice, rigidity in a certain part of the body means circulation decreases, lymphatic fluid becomes stagnant, and toxicity builds. When toxins build enough, dullness sets in and awareness diminishes, lessening aliveness in that part of the body.

Eventually, a dull part of the body becomes forgotten. Many people have parts of their bodies that are gray areas; that part of the body has been cut off from awareness. The nadis have become blocked.

The ancient teachings tell us that for pranayama to work most effectively, we need to purify our nadis:

> *When there is complete cleansing of the nadis, outward signs are observed. Among them, surely the lightness and luster of the body are obvious. With the cleansing of the nadis, the Prana can be restrained as is desirable.* (Hatha Yoga Pradipika, Chapter 2, Verse 19)

Purifying the nadis enlivens the whole body. The "lightness and luster" describe the external manifestations of this aliveness. **As vitality grows, inner awareness deepens as well, and that expanded awareness shows us the truth of what we feel.**

The text states that Prana can then be "restrained as is desirable," a teaching that is interpreted two ways, corresponding to the two definitions of Prana. The most common explanation, building on the definition of Prana as air, is that the yogi can hold his breath for a long time. The other interpretation, based on Prana as aliveness, is that we can channel emotions, rather than being driven by them. My anger, instead of being something to fight, becomes a fuel that propels me to do good. When the energies inside of us are in conflict, *we* are in conflict. **To restrain the Prana means having the ability to channel the flow of energy in a way that is productive or meaningful.**

> *Consequently, there is an increase in the fire in the abdomen, adequate expression of nada, and freedom from all diseases.* (*Hatha Yoga Pradipika*, Chapter 2, Verse 20)

"Fire in the abdomen" is sometimes translated as the digestive fire, meaning the workings of the digestive system. This definition is correct, but it means far more. **The fire in the abdomen is our vitality. It is our aliveness.** This ties into digestion, in that our digestion and absorption are optimal when the fire in the belly is strong. With optimal health comes increased vitality.

Many Hatha Yoga texts speak metaphorically of two abdominal fires. The first fire, *kamagni*, is felt by everyone; the second fire, *yogagni*, is felt only by yogis. Kamagni literally means "fire of pleasure" or "fire of passion," and refers to the animal energies we met earlier: anger, fear, and lust. They are called fires because they have the power to burn or melt ahankara. When anger is strong enough, for example, it can "melt" the rational self and cause a person to act like an animal. The ahankara maintains its stability by blocking the flow of fire or energy from the pelvis (ancient yogis saw all emotions as energy emanating from the pelvis). It does this by blocking the nadis in the belly, which dulls the energy, and by restricting breath, which reduces vitality.

The yogi strives to witness the abdominal fire without acting on it, then unblock the belly and breath and feel the fire in its fullest form, still without losing the witness. Kamagni witnessed in its fullest form becomes yogagni, the fire of yoga. It melts ahankara and gives the yogi the experience of universal oneness.

"Adequate expression of nada" means that the yogi can experience this flow of life everywhere, but can also turn down its volume in order to function using the mind, so the experience is uplifting but not overwhelming.

"Freedom from all diseases" refers to the idea that the yogi's body is so full of vitality that there is no room for disease. The body burns up illness as soon as it comes in. Whether or not that can really happen, we can't say, but that is the teaching.

Given that the nadis need to be purified in order to practice pranayama, the *Hatha Yoga Pradipika* provides two techniques to cleanse them: Anuloma Viloma, a pranayama taught in the final section of the book, and a group of yogic practices called the *Shatkriyas,* discussed in Chapter 4.

CHAPTER FOUR
SHATKRIYAS

The spiritual technology of the ancient hatha yoga tradition includes a set of cleansing techniques called the Shatkriyas. Most modern practitioners view these practices as physical purification alone. **We believe the effects of the Shatkriyas run much deeper than the physical.** We'll explore why by looking at the ancient intention for these practices and examining each technique in detail.

As you learn about the Shatkriyas in this chapter, please know that they may or may not be appropriate for you to practice. The traditional teaching is that a yogi needs to do these techniques in order for pranayama to be most effective, but we believe a practitioner can gain tremendous benfit from the pranayama techniques, with or without the Shatkriyas. The Shatkriyas will certainly alter one's experience of the pranayamas, adding a layer of depth and preparatory work, but we want to be clear that they are not essential in order to have a meaningful pranayama practice. You might practice one, all, or none of the Shatkriyas. We are introducing you to them here, and whether or not you explore them is up to you.

Literally six (*shat*) purifying actions (*kriyas*), **these practices were traditionally used to open a channel from the pelvis to the crown of the head.** Each kriya targeted a particular area of the body and opened a specific portion of that central channel. Once the channel was cleared from pelvis to crown, the yogi worked to guide energy into it.

We'll first examine Dhauti Kriya to understand this better.

Dhauti Kriya

Dhauti Kriya is the most intense Shatkriya, which requires the yogi to swallow a long, narrow cloth and remove it again. **The portion of the body that the practice opens is the chest and throat.** Yoganand's experience learning this technique sheds light on how it can work.

Yoganand

The day I learned Dhauti Kriya, I tasted the power of the Shatkriyas to transform and heal on all levels—physical, emotional, mental, and spiritual.

I had wanted to learn Dhauti Kriya for a long time, but the practice is so extreme that all the books insist upon an experienced teacher to guide a beginner. Since Swami Kripalu left his physical body before I could learn it from him, I held back from trying Dhauti Kriya until a visitor at the ashram agreed to teach me.

The year was 1985, and I walked into my new teacher's dimly lit room before the sun had risen. Two trays sat on the floor, holding a bowl, a teacup, a salt shaker, and a napkin. The display looked more like breakfast than preparations for an invasive yoga practice. My teacher unraveled the little ball of cloth that had been rolled up like gauze. Placing it in the bowl, he moistened it with water and sprinkled it with salt, and I began to burn with excitement. I watched eagerly as he prepared my cloth, and I wondered if I would walk out of the room a different person in some way.

My teacher explained the procedure, which sounded simple enough: Take the dampened cloth, 21 feet long and four inches wide, place one end in my mouth, and begin to swallow. Work for 20 minutes to swallow as much of the cloth as possible, then pull it out. The teachings say that after 20 minutes, digestive acids begin to burn the cloth.

With my teacher's encouragement, I placed one end of the cloth in my mouth and chewed it three or four times. It simultaneously generated saliva and a childhood memory of gnawing on paper out of boredom.

I suddenly remembered that I needed to swallow. So I swallowed, and a tiny bit of the cloth went down. It felt incredibly strange to swallow something and still have most of it hanging out of my mouth. I swallowed again, and suddenly I felt the cloth in my throat and panicked. A wave of nausea washed over me, and I began to gag. Out came the cloth.

Surprised and confused, I asked myself: How in the world am I going to do this?

I picked it up and started over a second, third, fourth time, gagging harder with each attempt. I tried an eleventh, twelfth time. The cloth tickled my throat, making it extremely difficult not to heave it back up. As I found myself consciously struggling to control my body's automatic reflexes, I began to feel a warm glow in my chest. Within a few more minutes, my eyes started to tear, and mucus ran down my face. I felt flushed and agitated. Again, I swallowed.

The 20-minute mark arrived, and my instructor told me to remove the cloth. I had only swallowed a foot and a half of the material, but I was exhausted.

I walked out of the room feeling inadequate as a yogi, since I so desperately longed to succeed in my practice and felt as though I failed at Dhauti Kriya. Shortly, however, the glow in my chest resurfaced. I noticed that deep within the muscle and tissue, my face, throat, and chest felt flushed and more open than ever before. I could feel my voice box, my glottis, and all of the structures of my throat. The intense work of the kriya stimulated these areas by releasing tension from the muscles and by cleaning the mucus and tear glands. For several hours, I felt an amazing aliveness in my chest and throat; then it faded once again.

Emotionally, I felt stronger after surviving the draining battle between my conscious mind and my automatic reflexes. Since swallowing the cloth interfered with my breathing, it activated my fear of dying and my fight-or-flight response. As I observed this fear without acting on it, my emotions shifted and I became more objective and less afraid. Thus, trying to swallow the cloth released emotional tensions.

The next morning I once again arose at 5:00 am and attempted the kriya a second time. I began to swallow the cloth, heaving and gagging, but it went down a little easier than the previous day. I felt it pass through my cardiac sphincter as it reached all the way down into my stomach. When my time was up, I realized that getting it out this time was much harder than the day before. When I pulled on the cloth, it tickled. When it tickled, my throat clamped down, preventing the cloth from moving anywhere.

The next moment deeply instilled in me the true value of a teacher. Once the throat clamps up, the cloth will not budge, even if the yogi pulls with both hands. That is scary! With no guidance, panic tells the novice to pull even harder. The cloth rubs against the soft lining of the throat and before long, the yogi pulls out four or five inches of bloody cloth. But my teacher simply instructed me to sip some salt water. My throat opened right up, and I could pull the cloth a bit further out of my mouth.

On the third day, I swallowed the whole cloth. For the rest of the day, I felt open and alive. I experienced a vivid image of a bright light shining in my chest, and like a flashlight, the warm glow reached up into my throat and head. I breathed with such ease, and when I swallowed, I felt my esophagus, my stomach, and every phase of the swallow in a way that I had never experienced before.

For the next month, I swallowed the cloth every single day, and I noticed that as the days passed, the charge began to diminish. Toward the end of the month, I put it in and took it out—no big deal. I stopped practicing the kriya for a month, then went back to it, hoping the profound effects would return after taking a hiatus. Still no charge. Today, 30 years later, I swallow the cloth once or twice a year, usually in demonstrations. I put it in, take it out, and it doesn't do a thing for me. I get more excitement from eating a french fry.

During a talk on the Shatkriyas, Swami Kripalu told his students, "Learn the Shatkriyas, then let them go." A lot of his disciples interpreted that to mean the Shatkriyas were not very important. I took it to mean this: Each Shatkriya opens the body in a particular way. Once the opening occurs, you have learned what you needed to learn from the kriya, and you can move on.

The *Hatha Yoga Pradipika* offers instructions for practicing Dhauti, which means both "cloth" and "to cleanse," in the following manner:

> *The yogi, according to the direction of his guru, should slowly swallow a wet piece of cloth which is four fingers wide (and 21 feet long,) and should pull out that piece of*

> *wet cloth. This is called Dhauti Karma.* (*Hatha Yoga Pradipika*, Chapter 2, Verse 24)

The *Gheranda Samhita* refers to a second version of this kriya, in which the yogi swallows water rather than a cloth:

> *Let the wise practitioner drink water full up to the throat. Then raise the Prana (through Agni Sara) and vomit out the water.* (*Gheranda Samhita*, Chapter 1, Verse 39)

Most of the Shatkriyas are invasive in nature, but Dhauti Kriya is by far the most extreme. It should therefore be approached with utmost sensitivity and respect.

Swami Kripalu told a story about a man who wanted to practice the Dhauti Kriya after reading about it in a book. Too shy to approach a teacher, he tried it at home. Once the cloth reached his stomach, it somehow tangled itself into a knot too large to pass back up through his cardiac sphincter.

Unable to remove the cloth from his body, the man panicked. He ran into the street, screaming and pulling on the cloth. Hearing his desperate cries, his relatives found Swami Kripalu in his meditation room and begged him to help.

"What is it?" Swami Kripalu asked. "I am meditating."

They cried, "Our relative is dying!"

"What happened?"

"He swallowed the cloth and it got tied into a knot. It's stuck!"

Swami Kripalu said, "Have him drink a cup of ghee and he will be fine." He then returned to his meditation.

The novice yogi drank the ghee, which made him vomit the cloth right up.

Because of his extensive experience, Swami Kripalu knew what the inexperienced yogi did not. The moral of the story: **The Shatkriyas require discrimination as well as the wisdom of a teacher who understands how they work, and what to do when they go wrong.**

Nauli Kriya

Nauli Kriya involves moving the abdominal muscles in a particular manner and **specifically works to open the belly area.**

> *Having bent the shoulders forward, rotate the abdominal muscles to the right then left quickly like a whirlpool. This practice is called Nauli Karma or Nauli Kriya.* (Hatha Yoga Pradipika, Chapter 2, Verse 33)

From a standing position, the practitioner inhales, then exhales as fully as possible. Holding the breath out, she places her hands on her thighs and lengthens her spine. This creates a vacuum in the belly area, where the abdominal muscles are pulled back strongly toward the spine. The yogi then works to peel those muscles away from the spine and move them in a rippling motion from left to right (or right to left). As the yogi continues and quickens the motion, it begins to feel as if the abdominal muscles are moving in a circle.

Moving the abdominal muscles in a circle churns the belly, bringing sensation and aliveness to the stomach, a part of the body we typically feel only in times of pain or discomfort. **The churning also releases tensions** held in the belly as a protective armor. We build this armor as a defense against feeling pain, but it often becomes chronic, causing illness and diminishing vitality. Nauli Kriya dissolves tightness in the belly, and, the freer the abdomen, the easier the practice of Nauli.

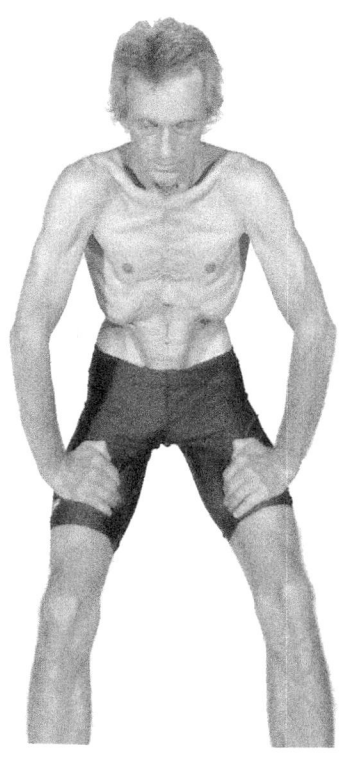

Nauli Kriya

Remember that, traditionally, once the yogi cleared the channel from pelvis to crown, he worked to guide energy into it. Nauli Kriya played an important role in that process, since opening the belly also began to free the pelvis. The pelvis contained a powerful energy source that manifested outwardly as anger, fear, and sex drive. The yogis wanted to funnel this energy inward and upward so it could enliven the whole body and flood the mind, enhancing the ability to think and perceive.

Because this was easiest when they were actually experiencing the anger, fear, or sexual desire, many of their practices—fasting, non-possession, pranayama, vigils—were created to intentionally make them what we might call "a little edgy." Whenever they felt this way, they worked to channel the energy out of the specific emotion and into an expression of greater aliveness inside the body.

Basti Kriya

Basti Kriya involves drawing water into the colon and expelling it. **Basti helps Nauli Kriya to open the belly, and carries that work down into the pelvis.**

> *In a squatting position, water up to the navel, with a tube inserted into the anus, contract the rectum so that water will be sucked inside. The washing of the organ of excretion is called Basti Karma. A bamboo tube six fingers long (six to eight inches) is called a Basti. Four fingers length of it (four to five inches) is inserted into the anus. Two fingers of length should remain outside.* (Hatha Yoga Pradipika, Chapter 2, Verse 26)

Historically, yogis performed this technique in a river, but it can be practiced in a bathtub as well. The yogi inserts the tube into her anus, exhales fully, and holds her breath out in external Kumbhaka. Stretching her waist, she slowly begins Nauli Kriya to churn the belly or gentle Agni Sara to pump the stomach. These abdominal movements pull water into the colon. As she continues working her abdomen, the process offers feedback that allows her to adjust the movements to draw more water into her body. Once the colon is filled with water, the yogi practices gentle twisting postures and then expels the water into a toilet.

Dry Basti entails the same procedure, except with air. The practitioner sucks air into her body through the tube, then expels it.

Fasting the day before Basti Kriya enhances the practice on several levels. Physically, the colon is more likely to be empty, which reduces the chance of blockage as the yogi pulls the water into her body. The abdomen, also less full after fasting, experiences heightened sensation, allowing the yogi to better attune to the practice. With the increased sensitivity, the yogi sometimes feels exactly where and how the water is moving in her body.

Working with the Shatkriyas, one is easily tempted to focus on the external achievement of the techniques and miss the depth of the practices.

Yoganand

I traveled to India for a training, and we had a Dhauti Kriya competition to see who could swallow the cloth the fastest. I swallowed the whole thing in three minutes and 45 seconds, so I finished in fourth place. The contest offers one approach to the Shatkriyas: Are you man enough? On a deeper level, the value of these practices is to help awaken, enliven, and energize particular parts of the body.

With Basti and Nauli, awareness of the belly and pelvis is heightened. The yogi sits in the tub, trying to draw the water in through his anus, and it simply will not flow into his body. He tries and tries, until one day he realizes that part of him *does not want* this water to come into his body. Acknowledging this resistance is the first step; the next step is to explore the resistance.

The yogi asks himself why he recoils from the experience, and the answer to this question almost always reveals fear. A tiny three-year-old voice says, "It might hurt." Once he recognizes this voice and the associated regression, the yogi stands in rich territory. He explores the voice further, and suddenly finds himself transported to a time in his childhood when he suffered from a digestive disorder that caused pain in the same area of the body used in the kriya.

The yogi then realizes that the water has not come into his body because *he has not allowed it to enter.* Understanding this, he knows he must choose to let the process happen. Slowly, he begins to let the water in, grows anxious, and tightens something inside his body. He pauses to ask himself what is tightening up. An image arises of a time when he felt pain, and he sees an association between that pain and the physical tightening to thwart the flow of water. If he can soften around the hurt so that the water can pass into his system, the potential for clearing out and healing is tremendous.

Whenever we look at places we have tightened to protect ourselves from real or imagined threats, we challenge our conditioning and open to the possibility of a new way of being.

Yoganand

Reading about the Shatkriyas in the ancient texts, most people interpret them exclusively as physiological purification. Folks believe that when the yogi swallows the big, long cloth, it rubs against the stomach wall and cleans the stomach. I personally don't believe this at all. The cloth is so soft, gauzy, and covered with mucus by the time it reaches the stomach, it sloshes around and has no ability to clean.

More than physical purification, the power of the Shatkriyas lies in energetically and emotionally opening the body. Students ask, why not do an enema instead of practicing Basti Kriya? During an enema, the person's abdomen passively allows the inward flow of water. By contrast, the yogi must willfully make Basti happen by activating muscles and using parts of the body in ways she does not ordinarily use them. **The stimulation shines light upon areas that usually remain in the dark.** An enema cleans the colon with no problem. Basti acts as a whole different animal because of the willful aspect. The yogi must figure out how to make the kriya happen. It's the difference between being pulled in a wagon and riding a bicycle; the experience shifts dramatically when one propels oneself.

After practicing Basti Kriya, the yogi knows her insides because she has felt them. The organs, tissues, and muscles no longer hide in the dark. That part of the body comes into the light.

Kapalabhati

Kapalabhati is a series of strong exhalations through the nose, each followed by a passive inhalation through the nose. **The primary part of the body it opens is the solar plexus region.**

The process of releasing and drawing in breath quickly as a bellows is well known as Kapalabhati. (Hatha Yoga Pradipika, Chapter 2, Verse 35)

Kapalabhati straddles the categories of kriya and pranayama, which can be confusing. It is a breathing exercise, making it seem like a pranayama, but it is classified as a kriya in the *Hatha Yoga Pradipika* and other texts. Kapalabhati began as a kriya, with a focus on cleansing and illuminating part of the body, and then evolved into *Bhastrika*, a more vigorous pranayama with an emphasis on energy activation.

As a kriya, Kapalabhati offers both physical cleansing and enlivening. The name Kapalabhati means "skull polishing," referring to cleaning the inside of the skull (the nasal passages). The strong exhale in Kapalabhati purifies the nasal passages by pushing mucus toward the nostrils to be expelled. It also dilates the nostrils, making it easier to breathe deeply. Beyond the nasal cavity, the lungs are purified through a complete exchange of air. This can give the practitioner a feeling of exhilaration as the lungs exchange gasses more freely from the fresh air.

Looking deeper, **Kapalabhati has a profound effect on the abdominal area.** Since Kapalabhati is a series of strong abdominal contractions, each followed by relaxation of the same muscles, it releases the "armor" in the belly and increases aliveness there. After practicing Kapalabhati, the belly should feel tired and open, with the usual tensions dissolved. **This openness of the belly allows the student to be more in touch with her feelings.**

The final section of the book teaches Kapalabhati in greater detail.

Tratak

*T**ratak* is focusing one's gaze on an internal or external object. **It opens the middle of the brow, or the third-eye area.**

> *A well composed and completely attentive yogi should, with a steady gaze, fix his eyes on the target until tears are shed. This is called Tratak by teachers of Yoga.* (Hatha Yoga Pradipika, Chapter 2, Verse 31)

With external Tratak, the gaze is focused on a target outside the body, such as the glow of a candle. With internal Tratak, the seated yogi focuses the inner gaze, especially after pranayama, on a specific point inside the body. The texts list 12 to 16 internal target points, called *adharas*, adhara points, or *marma* points. A typical list of 14 points is shown in Figure 9. (Some traditions teach that those points with the strongest charge became the seven chakras.)

If the yogi perceives the target as neutral, then deep absorption might be the primary experience. If the focal point holds meaning for the yogi, then feelings or images might emerge. **When this happens, Tratak opens the yogi to an expanded state, and the yogi's conditioning is revealed by what the mind does with the focal point in that open state.**

When the ancient yogis practiced internal Tratak, they opened themselves to the subtle mental and emotional impressions that arose. Any associations with the body part could trigger *samskaras*, or identities. **As they witnessed the process and welcomed whatever came to the surface, they**

opened themselves to greater self-awareness and self-acceptance.

Consider a yogi practicing internal Tratak by focusing on the navel. As he focuses on his belly button, he notices tightness in his abdomen. He relaxes the tightness, which allows fear to emerge and reminds him how much fear he feels in daily life. The softening of his abdomen also causes him to experience his belly as large, and he feels the pain of overeating. In the weakness in his belly, he senses his dissatisfaction with himself and his inability to be what he thinks he should be in life.

He continues focusing on his adhara, his navel, and watching whatever arises. Each of these observations becomes an opportunity to face and accept the truth, for the yogi to see not who he wants to be, but who he really is. **The ancient yogis wanted to live in truth, even if the truth felt unpleasant to the ego mind. When we can face our truth, we are more fully alive, rather than diminishing life to keep ourselves comfortable.**

Here is one way to practice Tratak: Move through each of the points listed in Figure 9, beginning with the lowest physical point, the big toes. Spend up to five minutes focusing on each point, then move to the next point. It will take a little over an hour to journey through all the points in the body. When done daily, the practices renders the inner world very real.

> Figure 9.
> Fourteen Adhara Points:
>
> Big toes
> Ankles
> Knees
> Base of thighs
> Anus
> Genitals
> Navel
> Heart
> Throat
> Tip of tongue
> Palate
> Tip of nose
> Point between eyebrows
> Crown of head

Neti Kriya

Neti Kriya is one of the more invasive kriyas and **works to open the nasal passages.** In the first of two methods, a string is fed through the nostril and pulled out of the mouth.

> *Great, adept people call that Neti in which the yogi pulls out of the mouth a soft string after having made it pass through the nostrils.* (Hatha Yoga Pradipika, Chapter 2, Verse 29)

Although the text refers to a soft string, a coarse string is often used, and it burns as it passes through the nasal cavity. The idea behind the rough string is physical purification. Since the string flosses the soft palate as it passes from the nasal passage through the mouth, it is believed to wipe away bacteria.

When Neti Kriya is practiced for reasons beyond the physical effects, a rubber catheter works well and causes no pain when done correctly.

Yoganand

When I lead advanced pranayama programs, I teach Neti Kriya using a sterile neoprene urinary catheter. I want my students to explore the invasive quality of the Shatkriyas, and since I focus more on the emotional and energetic experience than the physiological component, we work with the catheters rather than the abrasive strings.

The second version of Neti Kriya is called *Jala* or water Neti.

> *Pour water through the nostrils and spit it out the mouth.* (*Gheranda Samhita*, Chapter 1, Verse 58)

The text describes one form of Jala Neti, but there are actually three ways to practice it. In the simplest method, the yogi pours water into one nostril and tilts his head to the side so it runs out of the other nostril. A more advanced variation involves pouring water into one nostril and tilting the head at such an angle that it runs out of the mouth. In the third technique, the yogi fills the mouth with salt water and bends forward with the crown of the head toward the floor. The water runs up into the nasal passage and, by blowing out through the nose, the water blasts out. The last version is best practiced in the shower, since the fluid runs down the forehead into the hair.

Some students experience profound transformation when they practice Neti Kriya, but only when they soften into the technique and explore it rather than trying to accomplish it.

One student with a history of sexual abuse, whom we will call Anna, sat down to try Neti Kriya. At first, Anna fed the catheter through her nostril with ease, but before long, she began to regress. Fear from when she was four years old arose, and she suddenly found herself at the time of the abuse. Like the childhood encounter, the kriya was new and scary. It involved a foreign object entering her body and left her vulnerable, wondering what would happen.

Anna chose to sit with the experience, part of her feeling like the four-year-old child, afraid and confused, but another part of her remaining present, knowing it was a flashback. She reassured herself, "I am in a yoga program, and I am safe. I'm going to work with the feelings the Shatkriya is activating."

When the time came to reach her fingers into her mouth and grab the catheter, Anna felt the abuse happening all over again—except this time, she was the abuser. Since her childhood perpetrator abused her orally, she now felt that she was doing it to herself. Quite often, in the aftermath of an abusive situation, the survivor suffers fears such as "I might do that to someone else" or "It might happen to me again."

By containing the whole experience inside, Anna absorbed the roles of both the perpetrator and the victim. She completed the kriya and, after it was over, she shared how she had been empowered by it in that she was able to pull herself above the experience rather being consumed by it. She remained the adult yoga practitioner, at least partially, which kept her from dissolving into pieces of the past triggered by the kriya.

Yoga techniques stir up feelings—your greatness, worst fears, past traumas, inadequacies. If you can contain them, the yoga becomes a crucible in which transformative work can happen. Anna was able to contain her experience and do a piece of healing work with the feelings that surfaced. If, on the other hand, what comes up is more than the practitioner can integrate, then there is a possibility of re-traumatizing. In the latter case, it's better to recognize that you are not ready to delve into the issue.

The point of Neti Kriya and the other invasive kriyas is not to force an object into the body and then remove it. **The true worth lies in the energetic, emotional process of exploring the kriya—expanding to a point where you can allow invasion of the body to occur while remaining open to the increased aliveness, well-being, and self-knowledge that the practice offers.**

Yoganand

For many students, Neti Kriya begins long before they remove the catheter from its packaging. They walk into the first program session, see the catheter in the folder next to their seats, and they experience fear, vulnerability, excitement, or a full-blown fight-or-flight response. Many students feed the tube into their nasal passages, but never pull it out through their mouths. When the tube starts to go in, something inside them says, "No!" If students approach the kriya with sensitivity, they can play with that voice and learn from it, whether or not the tube enters their bodies at all.

Once the catheter moves through the nasal passage, it travels down into the throat, and the yogi must reach into his mouth and take it out. Students struggle with themselves, saying, "My mouth doesn't open that wide." Yes, it does—if they want it to.

No one learns all the Shatkriyas in one sitting. These techniques unfold gradually, and one can benefit from continual practice as long as there is something valuable there to work with. People return months after a program and say, "I still do Neti Kriya every morning." If we get something out of it, it is valuable. **When a practitioner sits in a flood of thought and emotion, that is when the kriya is working.** As in Yoganand's example, if the thought of the invasive technique can generate a charge even a week before trying it, that's something to explore. Likewise, the kriya can continue to work long after it has been practiced. Dreams and memories might show up or become more vivid. Feelings blocked by trauma or injury might begin to flow again. The kriya might work 50 times, and on the 51st time, when the practitioner inserts the catheter into his body and says, "No big deal," he knows he is done.

While there is some overlap, **each technique works to open a different region of the body, together building the channel from the pelvis to the crown of the head:** Basti opens the pelvis; Nauli awakens the stomach; Kapalabhati enlivens the solar plexus; Dhauti illuminates the chest and throat; Neti opens the nasal passages; and Tratak taps into the third eye. The kriyas shine light into the darkness of the body and illuminate it.

Figure 10: Each of the Shatkriyas opens a specific area of the body, with the six techniques together opening a channel from the pelvis to the crown of the head.

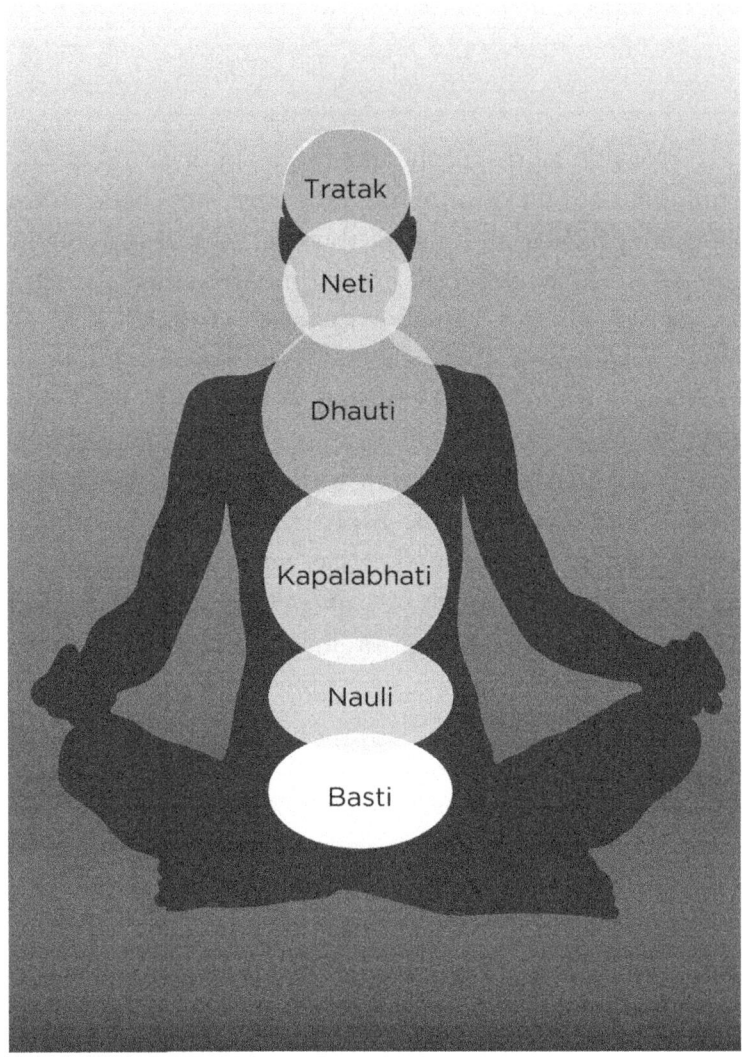

Shatkriyas and Fearlessness

Most of us spend our whole lives running from fear. We face it only when life forces it upon us, or when a goal renders the discomfort of fear worthwhile. **The ancient yogis, on the other hand, worshipped fear.** Swami Kripalu's guru was a man named Lakulisha, a well-known teacher in the age-old tradition called the *Pashupata Marga*.

The Pashupatas worshipped the Hindu God Shiva in the form of Rudra, who was the personification of fear at that time in history. As a spiritual practice, the Pashupatas sought out terrifying situations. Then they tried to reframe their terror to see it as the presence of god, or pure energy. Pashupatas would spend long stretches of time alone in isolated places—sleeping in abandoned temples or camping in cremation grounds. They believed that the more fear an environment evoked, the closer they were to god.

A Pashupata yogi who felt fearful might have said to himself, "I am afraid, but this fear is Rudra. It is God dissolving me by reaching out and pulling me into God." **They chased fear, and then worked to convert that fear into the experience of dissolving into oneness with spirit.** From the Pashupata viewpoint, fear was desirable.

By transforming fear into spiritual energy, the Pashupata yogis explored fearlessness. What if we did the same? What would it mean to have no trepidation? That does not mean that, if you encounter a snake in the road, you do not fear the snake; rather, **it means having no fear of yourself.**

Most of the time, we find ourselves divided between our fears and the things we want in life. Think of all the times in a given day that fear underlies a thought, feeling, or action: *I better not take that busy highway because the traffic is too heavy and I'll get into an accident. I can't walk past the ice cream shop because I won't be able to resist the temptation and I'll lose self-control. I can't go out with that person because I will get hurt, just like I did in the past.* We project our self-doubt onto the world and all of our experiences. **The Shatkriyas can help unravel that doubt, serving as powerful doorways to fearless living.** Through a process of chiseling away at the fear, not outright attacking it, we chip away little bits and pieces.

What fear do I hold in my throat and chest? Swallowing the cloth will illuminate it. Nauli, Kapalabhati, and Basti access the fear that resides in the belly and pelvic regions. Dread keeps those areas in darkness. **When we open them up, our inner radiance and profound well-being shines through, and we can realize our greatest potential in this life.**

To illustrate, think about a medical procedure. As the patient lies in a hospital bed, a stranger inserts a tube into his body, and the patient remains in the dark about what is happening. Afterward, he might say, "I will never go through this again," and build a tightness against it. The kriyas can help to heal and integrate that armor.

With a kriya, unlike a medical procedure, the yogi maintains control. Consider the difference between being shoved off a riverbank and choosing to jump into the water for a swim. The first scenario is filled with shock, the second with exploration. Practicing a kriya, we can stop and start when we wish. We can take it as far as we feel safe. The control lies entirely in our own hands.

The purpose of the action further distinguishes a kriya from a medical procedure. Even in the case of self-catheterization, in which the patient holds the reins, he inserts the tube into his body to achieve a focused goal: maintaining his health. If he inserts the same tube into his body for purposes of self-discovery, watching feelings arise, and increasing vitality and knowledge of his body, he creates a radically different experience. It is the difference between jumping in the river to save someone's life versus jumping in to leisurely float and play in the water. The intention behind the action colors the whole experience.

Yoganand

My understanding of the kriyas shifted one day in the dentist's office. I saw the drill, and I tightened up to protect myself from anticipated pain. Then I paused and asked myself, "What if I just let go and allow this procedure to happen? It will hurt, but that will be okay. Let me soften around it and stop resisting it." Suddenly, it became a spiritual experience, and I realized that, from major crises to minor occurrences, every life adventure holds the possibility for exploration and growth.

Think about a woman birthing a child. It is biologically intense and excruciatingly painful, but look at the spiritual possibilities of this profound event. **The potential to learn about ourselves in any situation is incredible, and the growth extends far beyond the physical body.** Whatever greets us, the learning is boundless, as long as we remain open to it. On the deeper levels—beyond stretching, strengthening, and feeling good—these are the invaluable treasures that yoga offers us.

CHAPTER FIVE
ASANA AND PRANAYAMA

Yoga is a journey, and pranayama is one stage of that journey. For any single stage to make sense, we must understand how it connects with the other segments of the journey. Patanjali describes yoga as having eight sequential parts: yama, niyama, asana, pranayama, *pratyahara, dharana, dhyana,* and *samadhi*. The *Hatha Yoga Pradipika* gives us four stages: asana, pranayama, mudra and meditation. Other texts give us different numbers of stages, but close inspection shows that they are describing the same path, just dividing it differently.

Universally, asana has always come before pranayama. The discipline of strengthening and steadying the body through asana prepares the student to purify ahankara and cultivate a steady witness. Then pranayama takes over and continues the work with ahankara and witness consciousness.

The *Hatha Yoga Pradipika* instructs:

After Asana practice becomes steady, the Yogi observing Yama and taking wholesome and measured quantities of food, should correctly practice Pranayama according to his Guru. (*Hatha Yoga Pradipika*, Chapter 2, Verse 1)

In the ancient traditions, asana laid the foundation for pranayama, and the relationship between asana and pranayama took three forms: 1) Asana prepared the student for pranayama, 2) The student learned ideal asanas for practicing pranayama, and 3) Asana and pranayama were woven together in advanced practice. We'll look at each of these more closely.

1. Asana prepared the student for pranayama. Postures prepare the student for breath work by beginning the process of **uncovering one's truth.** Anyone who has taken a yoga class knows that asana practice can elicit resistance. It reveals our weaknesses and fears, truths that arise in pranayama as well. **When we work to integrate these truths, we ultimately grow stronger and more confident.**

Asana practice also prepares the student for pranayama by **enhancing introversion**—inviting us to release external objects and events from our awareness and look inside, exploring our inner worlds.

In addition, asana practice **introduces us to the mind-body connection** or, as the hatha yogis saw it, the flow of Prana that underlies all thought, feeling, and action. Some variation of the following process happens for anyone who practices extended holdings in asana: The student enters Bridge posture, for example, and, at some point, the mind begins to find the posture repulsive. To escape, the mind focuses on something happening outside the body. As the student breathes deeply, the mind lets go of the external focus, and the student can focus on what the posture feels like. The teacher might facilitate this process by asking the student to focus on alignment details. As the student's attention grows more internal and the body begins to tire, specific sensations become more prominent. Soon the student's attention is so absorbed in those sensations that it couldn't break free if it tried.

Next, as the student continues to hold the posture, the physical sensations become emotionally charged, and the student wants to label them as discomfort or pain. If the student can remain a witness, resisting those labels, the emotion becomes simply energy, and the student's sense of self partially dissolves.

The initial practice of pranayama, particularly breath retention after pranayama, is an extension and refinement of this process in asana. In pranayama, the body is in a more restful position, so the intensity comes more from energy rushes and breath retention, and less from muscular stretch and exhaustion. Rather than being pulled into the sensation of stretched or working muscles, the attention is drawn to the feelings generated by holding the breath.

The practitioner experiences more of the "spaces" inside the body. Sometimes the belly feels empty like a vast landscape. The heart and lung region, as well as the pharynx and sinus cavities, can feel like mysterious spaces where anything could be felt. During the breath retention and immediately after a pranayama, the student can explore an inner world opened by the pranayama.

2. The student learned ideal asanas for practicing pranayama. When giving instruction in pranayama, the hatha yoga texts begin by telling the student to sit in a particular asana. They suggest the asana that most supports learning and increases the immediate benefit of the pranayama session.

The traditional asanas for pranayama instruction were *Padmasana* (lotus posture), *Siddhasana* (posture of mastery), and *Swastikasana* (swastika posture). These postures were recommended because some aspect of them made the pranayama practices easier to do or made the effects easier to feel. The students would practice pranayama in these postures until they were very comfortable with the techniques.

In modern yoga practice, we have found that these traditional positions can pose challenges for beginning practitioners. Lotus posture, for example, can create strain in the knees. For this reason, we suggest these positions only for advanced pranayama practitioners.

3. Asana and pranayama were woven together in advanced practice. When it comes to asana, the ancient teachings focus heavily on seated or supine postures in which pranayama can be practiced. The *Hatha Yoga Pradipika* teaches 16 postures, all of which are seated or lying positions. The *Gheranda Samhita* teaches 32 postures, also seated or lying postures, with the exception of two that might have been standing poses (this is unclear due to inconsistent use of Sanskrit names among yoga schools at the time). This is very different from our modern yoga classes, which often feature a great variety of standing poses.

Once pranayama was learned, it was practiced in every asana, often combined with extended posture holdings. The intensity generated by the posture was combined with the intensity of the pranayama and breath retentions. Asana faded into the background, becoming the setting for pranayama practice.

As the student progressed deeper into pranayama, the moments after each pranayama became more expansive. The ahankara dissolved more in the flow of energy released by the pranayama. This period of the practice grew longer, and pranayama faded into the background as meditation emerged.

Like a lotus flower unfolding its petals layer after layer, the stages of yoga unfold. The physical practice of asana opens to contain the energetic practice of pranayama. Pranayama unfolds to reveal the meditative practices of pratyahara and mudra. Mudra opens to reveal the states of profound dissolving that bring about the experience of universal oneness.

How to Sit for Pranayama

Here we turn to practical considerations about sitting comfortably for pranayama. Most important, **a practitioner should sit in a stable position with the torso vertical and elongated.** This will have the greatest impact on your experience and should be the focus when choosing a seated position. With this in mind, we recommend three positions for pranayama: 1) sitting cross-legged, 2) kneeling, or 3) sitting in a chair.

Sitting Cross-Legged

Traditionally, pranayama was practiced in *Sukhasana*, a cross-legged seated position with the torso vertical and straight. To explore this option for yourself, sit cross-legged on the floor without a cushion. Notice if you feel discomfort or pain in your ankles, knees, hips, or back. Discomfort in the ankles can often be eliminated by placing a loosely folded towel under them. Discomfort in the knees can be alleviated by placing folded towels, blankets, or pillows under them. The primary intention is to give your knees something to press into, so avoid propping your knees any higher than you need to.

Next, sit as straight as you can, and notice if your knees are higher than your hips, causing your back to round. If they are, your abdominal breathing will most likely be restricted. Sit on a folded blanket or cushion, and see if you can elevate your hips slightly higher than your knees. If you can do this while feeling completely stable, then a cross-legged position might work well for you. If you cannot comfortably do this, then kneeling or sitting in a chair is a better option for you.

Sitting cross-legged with a folded towel for support

Students with open hips might find that they can sit on the floor, torso straight, without a cushion. For pranayama, we still recommend using a small prop under the sacrum. Your abdominal muscles might be strong enough to hold you erect, but you will be able to breathe more deeply and with greater ease if the prop is doing some of the work.

Sitting in a Chair

All the pranayama techniques recommended in this book can be practiced while sitting in a chair; for students with ankle, knee, hip, or back issues, this might be the best way to practice. If you sit in a chair for pranayama, make sure that your feet can rest on the floor and your thighs on the seat of the chair. If the chair is too high and your feet dangle, your legs are more likely to tingle or fall asleep. If the chair is too low, your back will tend to round.

Sit with your back away from the back of the chair. Leaning back, even slightly, will cause your chest to drop and compress your abdomen, reducing the depth of your breath. If back support is essential for you due to weakness or injury, place a tightly rolled towel or yoga block between your low back and the back of the chair. Pressing into the prop will keep your chest open and reduce the work of sitting up straight.

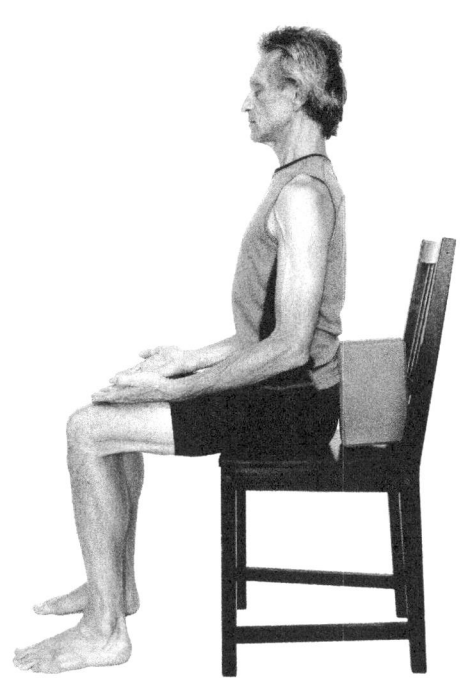

Sitting in a chair, with a block supporting the back

Kneeling

The traditional kneeling position is called *Vajrasana*, and provides an easy way to keep your torso straight and vertical. If you feel discomfort in your ankles or knees, try placing a rolled towel under them. To ease pressure on the knees, a folded blanket may be used between the buttocks and calves, or you can straddle a stack of cushions or folded blankets. Discomfort in the ankles can be reduced by separating them and letting them roll outward. If you cannot alleviate discomfort in your ankles or knees, try the other positions listed above.

Kneeling with a rolled towel under the ankles

We recommend these three positions for modern practitioners, since they best support your body and the practice of pranayama. The hatha yoga texts also describe advanced postures for pranayama that enhance abdominal and pelvic muscle engagement; these will be discussed in Chapter 7.

PART III

THE PRACTICE OF PRANAYAMA

CHAPTER SIX
PRANAYAMA TECHNIQUES

The Hatha Yoga texts describe two key purposes for practicing pranayama. First, **pranayama purifies the nadis**, or energy channels, making the body fully alive (see Chapter 3). Second, **pranayama invites energy into the central channel, or sushumna, causing ahankara to dissolve.**

To purify the nadis, we are given the shatkriyas, covered in Chapter 4, and the breathing exercise Anuloma Viloma. To direct energy into sushumna, the *Hatha Yoga Pradipika* offers eight kumbhakas or pranayamas: *Suryabhedana, Ujjayi, Sitkari, Shitali, Bhastrika, Bhramari, Murcha and Plavini.*

Three of these pranayamas—Suryabhedana, Murcha, and Plavini—are not safe according to current medical understanding. We will describe them here for historical perspective and understanding, but their practice is discouraged.

The other five pranayamas—Ujjayi, Sitkari, Shitali, Bhastrika, and Bhramari—are appropriate for most students, and thorough instruction will be given. We will also teach Dirgha to warm the body up for other pranayamas, Anuloma Viloma to purify the nadis, and the shatkriya Kapalabhati to raise energy. These eight techniques were taught by Swami Kripalu and are used in the Kripalu and Pranakriya traditions. We will cover them in the order that we would encourage students to practice them.

Each pranayama falls into one of four categories, based on its purpose: (1) warming up the body and mind, (2) purifying the nadis, (3) raising energy or awakening the sun, and (4) dissolving the mind (ahankara) into the witness or channeling energy into the moon. These categories are important because they convey the intention of each pranayama and give an idea of the effects you might feel from practicing them.

Figure 11. Eight pranayamas taught in this book, by category

Warming up the body and mind
1. Dirgha
2. Ujjayi

Purifying the nadis
3. Anuloma Viloma

Raising energy
4. Kapalabhati
5. Bhastrika

Channeling energy
6. Sitkari
7. Shitali
8. Bhramari

It should be noted that there are numerous variations for a given pranayama technique. According to Swami Kripalu, there are four to six hundred pranayamas, and the eight described in the *Hatha Yoga Pradipika* are not specific techniques, but rather categories of pranayamas. It is for you to determine which is the right variation for you. We can give you a place to start; the exploration is up to you.

Safety

The ancient yogis who gave us the pranayama techniques knew very little about anatomy. In their time, it was considered improper to touch a dead body, and surgery was practically nonexistent. Any knowledge they had of anatomy was intuitive. They believed their bodies to be full of winds, fires, and oils that pushed, burned, and flowed to create movement. Their answer to ailments was to generate more or less of these forces to bring balance. As modern practitioners, we have much more knowledge of anatomy, physiology and psychology to draw upon.

Ideally, all pranayamas should be learned from a skilled teacher. If you are a new student, our hope is that this instruction will support you in a basic practice until you have found a teacher who can guide you further. For experienced students, our hope is that this material will refine and enrich the techniques you have already learned.

As we cover each technique, we will address safety considerations specific to the technique. There are also general guidelines that apply to all techniques. **If you feel any of these symptoms, you should discontinue your pranayama immediately:** dizziness, headache, lightheadedness, slurred speech, numbness, or tingling in the lips, fingers, or feet. If the practice doesn't feel good in these or any other ways, don't do it.

Warm-up Pranayamas
Dirgha • Ujjayi

Just as the body needs to be warmed up for advanced postures, the body and mind need to be warmed up for advanced pranayamas. This reduces the risk of injury to the body, and increases the mind's ability to absorb energy. Otherwise, the mind tends to armor itself against energy. **Thus, the yogi wants to first prepare the body and mind to receive the energy, then raise it.**

Safety Awarnesses for Dirgha and Ujjayi

Dirgha and Ujjayi are usually safe for everyone to practice, but a few things should be considered. Dirgha and Ujjayi might not feel good if you have inflammation of the sinuses or throat. If excess mucus from a cold makes the pranayama difficult, do not strain. Any uncomfortable pressure in the abdomen from indigestion, colitis, hernia, or ulcers is a contraindication for practice, at least while the discomfort is present. If you have a cold or flu and are contagious, do not practice near others to avoid spreading your illness. Dirgha and Ujjayi pranayamas may be practiced while pregnant.

Dirgha Pranayama: The Full Yogic Breath

The first warm-up breath is Dirgha pranayama. Dirgha is not a classical pranayama, but has been adopted by many yoga traditions as a foundational breathing technique. **Its primary purpose is to prepare the body and mind for more vigorous pranayama practice.** You might also hear this pranayama called the Full Yogic Breath or the Three-part Breath.

The name Dirgha comes from Patanjali's *Yoga Sutra*, in which the author loosely defines pranayama as follows:

> *Pranayama is either outward, or inward, or balanced; it is regulated according to place, time, number; it is protracted and subtle.* (Chapter 2, Verse 50)

The term "protracted" here is translated from the Sanskrit word "dirgha," which means "stretched." This is commonly interpreted as "stretched in time," meaning slow or long, or "stretched in depth," meaning very deep. **Essentially, Dirgha pranayama is breathing as slowly and as deeply as you can, filling and emptying your lungs completely with each breath.** This stretches out all the breathing muscles and prepares the body for other pranayamas to come. In the same way that your body can move more gracefully into a posture when muscles have been stretched and tensions released, the pranayamas feel easier and more effective when the tensions have been released from the breathing muscles through Dirgha.

With regard to the mind, Dirgha is very soothing. You might feel yourself becoming calm after only a few breaths. Also, Dirgha begins the process of drawing the mind inward, since slow, deep breathing can only be done consciously. This introversion, along with increased sensitivity, makes the practice safer and more effective. This is because the yogi can discern the subtle effects of more vigorous pranayamas and determine which are positive and should be continued. This discernment is extremely important in the practice of breath retention, which is used in all advanced pranayamas. **Always practice Dirgha, along with the next pranayama, Ujjayi, to prepare your body for more advanced pranayamas.**

Dirgha can be practiced at any time of the day or night, but might feel uncomfortable immediately following a meal. Some practitioners find that practicing at bedtime makes it easier to fall asleep or deepens sleep.

Dirgha is very relaxing, especially for the shoulders and abdomen, which might have positive effects on digestion and elimination. Dirgha also calms the mind, and facilitates a complete exchange of air in the lungs. Dirgha can be helpful after breathing stale or smoky air and after stressful situations.

Pranayamas are not just breathing exercises; they are energetic experiences that we must feel deeply in order to fully experience their effects. **Done properly, Dirgha pranayama should pull the mind down into the body.** With its practice, we should find that sensations become more real to us and thoughts fade into the background. The body and mind should begin to merge.

Dirgha Technique

Dirgha is practiced by slowly inhaling and exhaling as fully as you can. Although this is usually done in an upright seated position, we will begin with a preliminary exercise lying down. The reason Dirgha is usually practiced upright is because twisting, forward bending, back bending, and standing will engage waist muscles and reduce the depth of breath. Lying on the back limits shoulder and rib movement and thus restricts breathing. However, deep breathing in any position that stretches breathing muscles can be used as a preparation for the formal seated Dirgha breath.

Dirgha Preliminary Exercise Lying Down

1) Tightly roll a yoga mat into a tube and lie over it as shown. Make sure your head is supported so your neck muscles can relax. Your shoulders should drape over the sides of the mat, and the end of the mat should be directly behind the bottom of your sternum so your belly is unsupported. In other words, only your head and ribs should be lifted, while every thing else hangs.

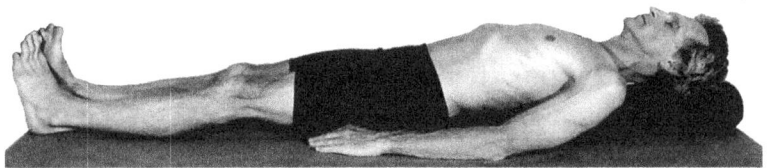

Lying position over a yoga mat

2) Place your palms lightly over your belly with fingers above and below your navel. Feel the warmth and pressure of your hands and begin to breathe so that your hands lift with your inhalations. Do not push your belly into your

hands; rather, feel the lift of your abdomen caused by your diaphragm muscle engaging. After several breaths, begin to deepen the inhalations and increase the movement of your belly. Grow the abdominal breath to be as deep as it can be.

Palms over the belly to feel it rise and fall
with the breath

3) Inhale your fullest abdominal breath and hold it in for 10 to 15 seconds. When you release the holding, let your hands relax to your sides, and lie still for a few natural breaths. Notice any ways in which your belly feels different after the abdominal breathing.

4) Press your palms lightly against the sides of your ribs. Try to have your whole palm in contact with your ribs, with your fingers pointing in any direction that is comfortable for your wrists. As you breathe, feel the pressure of your palms against your ribs and begin to breathe in such a way that your ribs expand into your hands. If you do not feel your ribs moving with your breath, you can inhale until your belly feels full and then hold your breath and pull your belly in against your spine. This will force the air to expand your ribs. Once you have felt the movement, you might be able to recreate it by breathing into the ribs and deepening it. Create as much movement in your ribs as possible.

Palms on the ribs to feel them expand with the breath

5) Inhale to expand your ribs as wide as you can and hold your breath for 10 to 15 seconds. When you release the holding, let your hands relax to your sides and lie still for a few natural breaths. Notice any ways in which your chest and waist feel different after the rib, or intercostal, breathing.

6) Bring your fingertips to press lightly against the top of your sternum. Your thumbs can rest on your collarbones. Begin to breathe so that your sternum lifts, and grow the movement as much as you can. If you do not feel your sternum lifting, you can inhale until your belly feels full and then hold your breath and pull your belly in against your spine. This will force the air to lift your sternum. Once you have felt the movement, you might be able recreate it by breathing into the upper chest and deepening it.

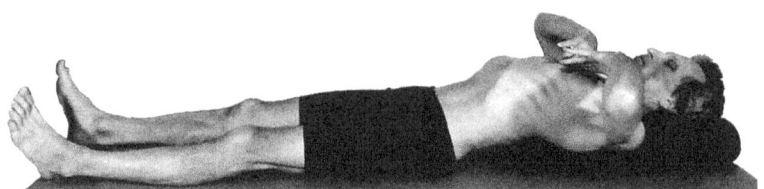
Fingertips on the sternum to feel it lift with the breath

7) Breathe to lift your sternum as high as possible, and hold your breath in for 10 to 15 seconds. When you release the holding, let your hands relax to your sides and lie still for a few natural breaths. Notice any ways in which your chest and shoulders feel different after the sternum, or clavicular, breathing.

8) Now combine the belly, rib, and chest breaths into one breath in the following manner: Exhale until you are empty of breath. Slowly inhale so that your abdomen lifts and, when it won't lift any more, continue breathing in to flare your ribs. When your ribs feel stretched wide, continue inhaling until your sternum is fully lifted. Hold in a few seconds and then let the breath flow out. At the end of the exhale, squeeze your belly fully. Repeat several Dirgha breaths. Don't worry about emptying from the top down. Simply let the air flow out naturally and then squeeze empty at the end. If you feel dizzy or nauseous, stop and breathe normally until you feel better.

9) After 10 breaths, relax completely and feel the effects of breathing deeply and releasing tension from your breathing muscles.

Practicing Dirgha Pranayama

Whereas the preliminary exercise above was practiced lying down, formal Dirgha is practiced in a seated position.

1) Sit comfortably in a cross-legged position, kneeling, or on a chair, as described in Chapter 5. Wobble a little side to side and back to front to make sure your seat provides adequate and balanced support. If your seat does not support you properly, your abdominal muscles will have to work harder and will be less available for breathing.

2) Bring your body to stillness. Feel your spine, and lengthen it as much as possible by pulling your tailbone down and the back of your neck up. Pull your shoulders forward and up, and then back and down. Pull your shoulder blades slightly in toward your spine and down toward your sacrum but keep your spine long.

3) Begin abdominal breathing. Keep it slow and explore how much movement you can create in your belly with your breath. When you exhale, pull your belly in as far as you can without straining. You might find it helpful to place your palms over your navel to feel your belly expand.

Palms on the belly to feel the full abdominal inhalation

Pulling the belly in for a complete exhalation

4) After five abdominal breaths, shift to intercostal (rib) breathing. As you inhale, flare your ribs as wide as you can. With each exhale, pull your ribs back in. You might find it helpful to place your hands on your ribs to feel them expand.

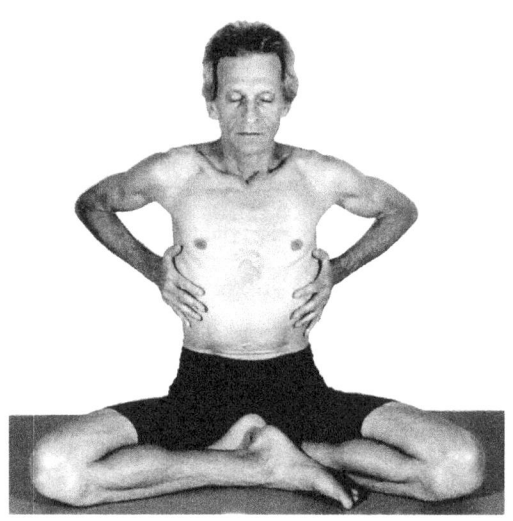

Palms on the ribs to feel them flare out during intercostal (rib) breathing

5) After five intercostal breaths, shift to clavicular (upper chest) breathing. If your shoulders need to move with your sternum, allow them to do so. Again, place your hands on your upper chest to feel the movement, if that is helpful.

Hands on the upper chest to feel it lift during clavicular (upper chest) breathing

6) After five clavicular breaths, transition to full Dirgha pranayama. Squeeze all the breath out without rounding your back and then, in one long breath, inhale into your abdomen, then your ribs, and then your sternum. Inhale as fully as you can and then relax and let all the breath flow out. Squeeze empty and repeat.

7) After five Dirgha pranayama breaths, return to your natural breath. Let your attention drift into your body and feel the effects. Take at least three to five minutes to explore all the changes in your body, emotions, and mind.

Growing into Dirgha

When first learning a new physical skill such as dance, martial arts, or yoga postures, the student is usually given a basic version of the technique. As the student masters the basic technique, the teacher adds details that lead the student to more advanced versions. Bridge posture becomes Wheel, for example.

With an asana or pranayama, the student is usually taught a basic version with a focus on safety. When the student is comfortable with the basic technique and safe alignment, the teacher will lead the student into a more advanced variation. Staying safe might require more skill or strength. It might also mean going deeper into the technique, breathing into tight areas or feeling the vulnerability that comes as the body opens. It might mean focusing on a feeling as it transforms from physical sensation to emotion to energy.

Going deeper might mean using devotional imagery, prayer, or visualizations. Historically, these were either intuitive techniques developed by the student or traditional tools passed on by the teacher. Some were handed down within yoga schools for many generations.

Once the student is comfortable practicing basic Dirgha pranayama as described above, the following techniques may be added. They require more effort and skill but, when mastered, create a deeper experience. They might seem to have little effect at first, but their practice makes a profound difference in more advanced techniques later on.

1) Spinal elongation. Most teachers encourage students to sit up straight for pranayama. This allows the student to sit longer without experiencing discomfort in the back, shoulder, or neck muscles. It also frees the abdomen so that deep breathing is easier.

This can be taken farther for a more esoteric effect. Sit as you normally would for pranayama. Wobble from side to side and front to back to make sure your cushion or chair is supporting you. Let your torso become still and place your hands on your hips. Press your hands down onto your hips and lift your ribs as high as you can above your hips. See if you can lengthen as much through your back as through your belly. Hold your ribs lifted, release your hands to your lap or knees, and breathe.

You will probably feel a stretch or tightness in your belly that might make it a bit more difficult to breathe deeply. These sensations are your psoas and lumbar muscles engaging and your abdominal muscles stretching. Stay long and feel these sensations. They might pull your attention down into your abdomen and pelvis.

Breathe deeply and you might notice that your breathing feels different. It takes more effort, but you might find your belly moving down and out when you inhale, and in and up when you exhale. There could be more movement in your ribs, too. They might flare out to the sides as you inhale, and the floating ribs might be pulled under as you exhale.

Soon, you will become tired and need to release this spinal elongation. Notice if your belly feels more open after releasing. Notice also if you feel more internal, and more aware or "grounded" in your core.

The attention being pulled into the abdomen and pelvis, the sensation of engagement and stretch in the abdominal and pelvic muscles, and the increased movement in the abdomen as you breathe all contribute to the introvertive effects of Dirgha pranayama. Practiced regularly for weeks or months in this way, Dirgha prepares the student for the root lock or *Mulabandha* mudra and the stomach lock or *Uddiyanabandha* mudra, which we will discuss in Chapter 7.

When you sit for Dirgha pranayama, don't just sit up straight—*elongate fully.* You can press your hands down on your hips if that enhances your elongation. Hold the elongation as you practice. If your elongation muscles become tired before you finish practicing Dirgha, release the elongation and continue the pranayama. After a breath or two, elongate again. Rest as often as you need as you practice the pranayama.

2) Breath retention. How a student experiences breath retention is a good measure for how open the student's nadis are. Holding for even a short period of time can generate fear-producing thoughts, such as, "What will I do if I need to breathe before the teacher tells me to?" If the student becomes caught up in these reactions, you could say they are not experiencing breath retention but rather the *reaction* to breath retention. They are more influenced by their mind and emotions, less by their body. A yogi would say that this student's nadis are not very open.

A more experienced student would witness the inner storm of thought and emotion, without reacting to it. At the same time, he would stay connected to his physical body and watch for sensations that indicate the body's real need for breath. An advanced practitioner might hold his breath until the witness dissolves and then immediately end the retention, strengthening their witness. **The more open the student's nadis, the more intense the inner experience that can be witnessed.**

When you are ready to end your practice of Dirgha pranayama, inhale fully and hold. Relax into the holding, but stay elongated. The elongation will try to pull your attention down into your abdomen and pelvis. The fear will try to pull your attention up into your head. The biological need to breathe will arise from your pelvis. Do not hold past the point where you lose the witness. **Instead of trying to hold your breath longer, practice holding your witness longer.**

3) Affirmations. Dirgha pranayama raises our energy, and that increased energy begins to dissolve the ahankara. We experience this dissolving as more space between our thoughts and less intensity around both thoughts and feelings. Things that felt very important to us no longer hold that intensity, and a small sensation can feel extremely profound.

Metaphorically, this is like a sugar cube being dropped into water. Ahankara is the sugar cube and high energy is the water. As the sugar cube dissolves, each sugar molecule moves away from the others. What was once rigid becomes fluid, and what was held at a specific distance is free to move close or drift away.

With the ahankara so malleable due to heightened energy, strong thoughts or prayers can have a powerful effect. When ego is rigid, an affirmation might have little effect. But, in the softness produced by the pranayama, ego can more easily shift in the direction the affirmation provides.

With Dirgha pranayama, affirm on the inhalation that you are opening to something positive. Affirm on the exhalation that you are releasing its opposite. For example, on the inhalation, say to yourself, "I open to my whole self." On the exhalation, say, "I let go of everything that keeps me small."

4) Visualizations. Many hatha yoga texts prescribe visualizations during pranayama. They usually contain sounds, shapes, or structures that were once symbols of spiritual safety or power. With the passage of time and change of culture, much of their power has been lost.

Visualizations work for some people but not others. If you wish to use visualizations with Dirgha, **use an image that supports the intention of Dirgha to calm the body and mind.** For example, if the ocean brings you peace, picture an ocean wave swelling on the inhalation and receding on the exhalation. You could also picture a serene image such as a still lake or a single blade of grass. If there is a symbol that holds safety or calmness for you, that might work as well. The point here, again, is to experiment and find what helps you deepen the intention of the practice: to calm the body and mind.

Once you're extremely comfortable with Dirgha pranayama, you can combine it with the next technique, Ujjayi. It's best to get really well established with Dirgha first. Otherwise it's easy to let Dirgha slip away when you move into Ujjayi, and the most profound effects come from practicing the two together.

Ujjayi Pranayama: Victorious Breath

The name Ujjayi means to "be victorious over" or "to conquer." In brief, Ujjayi pranayama is practiced by partially closing the glottis and vocal cords as you breathe, to produce a low-pitched hissing sound. The attractiveness of the sound pulls the mind away from thoughts and external situations, creating introversion. The mind is "conquered" by the sound.

> *With the mouth closed, gradually draw in the Prana through both nostrils from the throat, making a rasping sound that reaches into the chest. This Kumbhaka (breath restraint) named Ujjayi should be practiced while walking, standing, and going about. (Hatha Yoga Pradipika, Verses 51 and 53)*

Earlier, we learned that pranayamas are divided into four types: 1) pranayamas to warm up the body and mind; 2) pranayama to purify the nadis; 3) pranayamas that awaken the sun or raise energy; and 4) pranayamas that channel energy into the moon or dissolve the mind (ahankara) into the witness.

Ujjayi can be practiced either as the first type, a warm-up pranayama, or the fourth type, an energy-channeling pranayama. As a warm-up pranayama, Ujjayi is most effective when combined with Dirgha pranayama. As the text indicates, it can also be practiced "while walking, standing, and going about." It can also be practiced while doing asanas, as is common in Kripalu Yoga.

When you first practice Ujjayi, the mind might not cooperate. It might linger on something that just happened or jump ahead to ideas about what comes next. The mind could also be restless from moving at a fast pace. When the practitioner begins practicing Ujjayi, the sound begins to interfere with thinking and, if the student can make the sound louder than the thoughts, the thoughts will gradually subside. **Just as Dirgha pranayama dissolves tension in the breathing muscles, the Ujjayi sound dissolves thoughts in the mind.**

After 10 deep breaths with Ujjayi, the mind will become more still and more connected to the body. This makes any pranayamas that follow more safe.

As an energy-channeling pranayama, Ujjayi is practiced after energy-activating pranayamas, when the mind is expanded and the body full of energy. In that open state, the mind can easily get lost in the sound. A few rounds can take the student so deep that all external awareness disappears and the mind (ahankara) dissolves into the witness. This could lead to states of deep stillness or to transcendent awareness, which the ancient yogis described as the sun and moon uniting.

The benefits of Ujjayi are that it generates introversion, increases sensitivity, and brings you into the moment. This gets you more in touch with your emotions and physical body, and helps you stop fighting the mind. It helps you let go of disturbing experiences in the world, such as a difficult day at work. Ujjayi also calms the mind and nervous system.

> **Just as Dirgha pranayama dissolves tension in the breathing muscles, Ujjayi dissolves thoughts in the mind.**

Ujjayi Preliminary Exercise

Sit with your eyes closed and imagine that you are sitting in front of a mirror. Imagine that you want to fog the mirror. Inhale deeply and then open your mouth wide. Exhale slowly but strongly, with your lips a few inches from the imaginary glass. As you do this, listen to your sound. Repeat this several times.

Now fog the imaginary glass again, but this time through your nose. As you do this, try to keep the sound down in your throat, even though the breath is coming through your nose.

When the sound is strong and steady on the exhale, try making the same sound on the inhale. When the sound is steady and equally intense on the inhale and the exhale, you are ready to combine Ujjayi pranayama and Dirgha pranayama.

Practicing Ujjayi Pranayama

1) Sit comfortably in a cross-legged position, kneeling, or on a chair, as described in Chapter 5. Wobble a little side to side and back to front to make sure your seat provides adequate and balanced support. If your seat does not support you properly, your abdominal muscles will work harder and be less available for breathing.

2) Bring your body to stillness. Feel your spine and lengthen it as much as you can by pulling your tailbone down and the

back of your neck up. Pull your shoulders forward and up, and then back and down. Pull your shoulder blades in toward your spine and down toward your sacrum, while keeping your spine long.

3) Begin Dirgha pranayama as a base for Ujjayi. You might grow into Dirgha with several successively deeper breaths or go right to your deepest inhalation. Empty your lungs completely each time you exhale.

4) When you are comfortable with Dirgha pranayama, add Ujjayi. Start by making the sound on an exhale, as that is usually easier than the inhale. Once you add the sound to the inhale, try to keep the sound equally strong on both the inhale and exhale.

5) After 10 cycles of breath with the Ujjayi sound, release all control of your breath. Let your attention drift into your body, and feel the effects. Take at least three to five minutes to explore all the changes to your body, emotions, and mind.

Growing into Ujjayi

The techniques described below enhance the effects of Ujjayi and generate more of the pranayama's meditative (moon-dissolving) effects. They can be used when practicing Ujjayi as a warm-up, but might be hard to practice if you are not in a seated position. They will also have a greater impact if practiced after doing sun-activating (energy-raising) pranayamas.

1) Intensity of the sound. If you are new to Ujjayi, make the sound as loudly as possible. This requires a commitment to the pranayama that overcomes timidity. Once you are comfortable with the strong sound, try making a soft, barely perceptible sound. When the mind has turned inward, the barely perceptible sound can fully absorb the mind.

A more advanced technique is to practice making the sound just a little stronger than your thoughts. This becomes a game in which the mind tries to escape the sound, and the sound tries to confront the mind. The duel between mind and sound can cause the external world to disappear.

2) Resisting the breath. Tighten your throat enough that you have to work hard to push the breath out and pull it in. This makes the sound strong and absorbing. It also safely strengthens the breathing muscles.

3) Breath retention. Add a short breath retention after the inhale or exhale. The contrast between the strong sound and the silence between breaths can captivate the mind. Holding the breath in tends to be more absorbing than holding it out. This is because internal holdings feel comfortable longer than external holdings. When holding in, the need to breathe rises slowly; holding out, it rises quickly and can leave your mind a little disturbed. Only practice this way if you can fully calm your mind with the Ujjayi sound on the next round. During breath retention with Ujjayi you could try:
- Simply sitting and feeling the quietness
- Counting slowly to keep your mind focused
- Silently chanting a mantra, prayer, or affirmation
- Practicing a visualization

4) Combining Ujjayi with other pranayamas. Ujjayi can be combined with any other slow pranayama. As a warm-up, we add it to Dirgha pranayama. It can also be used with the slow pranayamas that come later in this chapter: Nadi Shodhana, Anuloma Viloma, Shitali, or Sitkari. It can also be used after breath retention. You can exhale with Ujjayi as you release the breath retention, or you can release first, allow your breath to regulate, then move into a couple minutes of Dirgha and Ujjayi.

To review, Dirgha and Ujjayi prepare the body and mind for the pranayamas that follow by 1) warming up the breathing muscles; 2) preparing the mind to receive energy; and 3) increasing introversion and sensitivity so the advanced practices are safer and more effective. Once you are extremely comfortable with Dirgha and Ujjayi, you're ready for the more advanced techniques in the sections that follow.

Pranayama for Purifying the Nadis
Anuloma Viloma

This book began with the story of Swami Kripalu entering into the mystical experience of yoga through Anuloma Viloma, the only pranayama that his teacher taught him. **Anuloma Viloma purifies the nadis and makes Prana flow into sushumna** (the central channel). Remember, these are the two purposes for practicing pranayama, according to the *Hatha Yoga Pradipika*.

Anuloma Viloma is a modern name used by Swami Kripalu and several other teachers. The *Hatha Yoga Pradipika* calls this pranayama Nadi Shodhana (nadi meaning "channel" and shodhana meaning "to purify") since this is the pranayama for purifying the nadis.

Some traditions call this pranayama Surya Bedhana, which is actually the name of a different pranayama that we will discuss later. It seems the two techniques go by the same name because of vague descriptions in the ancient texts.

Anuloma Viloma is also called *Sahita Kumbhaka*, meaning broken or interrupted breath retention. The practitioner inhales and holds, breaks the hold to exhale, then inhales and holds again. All of these names refer to the same practice as distinguished by different yoga schools.

> Anuloma Viloma also goes by the names:
> - Nadi Shodhana
> - Surya Bedhana
> - Sahit Kumbhaka

In short, Anuloma Viloma is inhaling through the left nostril, holding the breath in, then exhaling through the right nostril. The sequence is then reversed: inhale through the right nostril, hold the breath in, and exhale through the left nostril. The name Anuloma Viloma means "with the grain and against the grain." This is a reference to one nostril usually being more open than the other. Breathing through the more open nostril is breathing "with the grain" and breathing through the less open nostril is breathing "against the grain."

Swami Kripalu was adamant that Anuloma Viloma was extremely important and that all yogis should learn it early in their pranayama studies. This is because, when practiced correctly, it introduces the practitioner to all the processes that will be encountered on the pranayama path: heightened sun energy activated by the breath retention and the sweet flow of sensation that comes with slowly releasing the breath. As one repeatedly practices oscillating between the intensity of breath retention and the relief of the exhale, the reaction to each gradually minimizes, and the practitioner becomes able to sit with increasingly strong sensation.

In this process, the nadis are purified, and the witness for inner experience grows strong and steady; the practitioner learns to watch intense energy and emotion without reacting to it. It's important to distinguish here that being present to intensity by shutting down is not the true witness. To be fully open, even vulnerable, and not react is the true witness.

The *Hatha Yoga Pradipika* considers this conditioning essential in order for pranayama to have its full effect. The energy-activating pranayamas stir up emotion and passions. The full benefit comes in witnessing this process, without becoming restless or judgmental or turning the attention outward.

Another way of looking at purification of the nadis is that the student's prana (attention flowing inward) grows strong and apana (attention flowing outward) becomes weak. When our attention flows outward, it increases our identification with the outer world. When our attention flows inward, we have the experience of being part of something beyond our ego mind.

> To be fully open and vulnerable and still not react is the true witness.

Over time, the traditional Anuloma Viloma evolved into something quite different than what we've just described, as the Kripalu School of Yoga and other traditions reduced or eliminated the breath retention. What is often taught today is a meditative breath done through alternating nostrils. This can be calming and balancing, but it's completely different from the original practice. In the Kripalu tradition, the pranayama without the breath retention came to be called Nadi Shodhana, and the pranayama with the breath retention was called Anuloma Viloma.

Here, we are teaching the traditional pranayama, with the breath retention, as it was originally taught in the *Hatha Yoga Pradipika*.

Anuloma Viloma Technique

The *Hatha Yoga Pradipika* uses the name Nadi Shodhana for Anuloma Viloma and describes it in the following way:

> *The Yogi seated in Padmasana should draw in the Prana through the moon Nadi (left nostril) and having retained it according to his capacity, should release it through the sun Nadi (right nostril).* (Chapter 2, Verse 7)

The above verse tells us to inhale through the left nostril, hold to our capacity, then exhale through the right nostril.

> *Again, drawing in the Prana through the sun Nadi, he should inhale to his capacity and hold the Prana in the abdomen. Having systematically and correctly performed Kumbhaka (breath retention), he should release it through the moon Nadi.* (Chapter 2, Verse 8)

Here we are told to repeat the sequence going the other way, and we learn more about the inhalation and holding. The text says to inhale to our capacity, which means inhale fully enough to feel a stretch in the belly. Our holding must be systematic, which means we must be able to repeat it again and again. If you hold your breath too long on one side, your retention will be shorter on the other side. Holding to capacity, then, is the longest you can hold without compromising the sequence on the other side.

> *Through that particular Nadi which Prana is released, draw in the Prana again. Retaining it with much effort, he should slowly release the Prana using the other nadi. He should not release forcefully or quickly.* (Chapter 2, Verse 9)

Here the technique is summarized, and we learn that we are to hold with "much effort." The effort comes from finding the fine line between holding as long as we can and maintaining the length of the holding on the other side. This requires incredible discernment. This verse also tells us we must be able to exhale slowly and with control. This helps ensure that we don't hold too long, in which case we'd need to exhale sharply. **Through the breath, we are building strong energy and challenging the mind to stay present so that releasing the breath is a conscious choice, not a reaction.**

> *If one draws in the Prana through the moon Nadi, one should release the restrained Prana through the sun Nadi. If the Prana was drawn in by means of the sun Nadi, after the holding, the Prana should be released by means of the moon Nadi. As a result of the regular practice of this process, the mass of many Nadis becomes unified within three months.* (Chapter 2, Verse 10)

The practice done properly will cause the nadis to "unify" or fully open within three months. According to this text, when all the nadis open, they merge to become the sushumna nadi (central channel). This is the sun and moon uniting. This is prana and apana ascending as one energy.

> *In the morning, at noon, and in the evening, one should offer the practice of Kumbhaka gradually building up to eighty breaths.* (Chapter 2, Verse 11)

We are told to practice three times each day. Some versions of this text indicate four times, adding a midnight practice. Eighty breaths, or 40 rounds, takes about an hour for most people. So the traditional teaching is to practice three or four hours of Anuloma Viloma each day for three months to purify our nadis and prepare in the best way for the pranayamas that follow.

Remember that this text was written for yogis who dedicated their lives to this practice. For most of us, a slower approach is more appropriate, and you can benefit from practicing Anuloma Viloma even once a day. There are those who train for marathons and those who benefit from running a mile. Still, it's inspiring to know the history, tradition, and possibility.

The benefits of Anuloma Viloma are an increased capacity to be with experience, especially uncomfortable experience; a stronger sense of self that is separate from thoughts, feelings, and events; increased introversion; a profound sense of meditative awareness, which creates an easier transition to meditation or asana practice; a sense of increased spaciousness and expansiveness; and greater distance from events happening before the practice. There is research, mostly from India, showing that Anuloma Viloma balances the two hemispheres of the brain. While we believe this could be true, the research is questionable.

Practicing Anuloma Viloma Pranayama

1) Sit comfortably in a cross-legged position, kneeling, or on a chair, as described in Chapter 5. Wobble a little side to side and back to front to make sure your seat provides adequate and balanced support. If your seat does not support you properly, your abdominal muscles will have to work harder and be less available for breathing.

2) Bring your body to stillness. Feel your spine and lengthen it as much as you can by pulling your tailbone down and the back of your neck up. Pull your shoulders forward and up, then back and down. Pull your shoulder blades in toward your spine and down toward your sacrum, but keep your spine long.

3) Begin Dirgha pranayama. You may grow into Dirgha with several successively deeper breaths or go right to your deepest inhalation. Empty your lungs completely each time you exhale. Add the Ujjayi sound to help keep your mind focused.

4) Practice Dirgha pranayama for about two minutes, until it feels absorbing and there is no resistance. Then, raise either hand to your face and, when you start your next exhale, block the right nostril so that all the breath flows out slowly through your left nostril. You can continue making the Ujjayi sound if you wish. As soon as you are empty, inhale through your left nostril and immediately exhale through your right. Continue alternating breaths through your nostrils (exhale, inhale, change; exhale, inhale change, etc.)

until your mind has relaxed into this level of practice (about four rounds). Make sure the breath is as deep as it can be. If you feel dizzy or nauseous, slow down. You can use any comfortable hand position to block your nostrils; the yoga tradition recommends Vishnu Mudra, shown here.

Vishnu Mudra

Anuloma Viloma with Vishnu Mudra

5) After about five cycles of Dirgha pranayama through alternate nostrils, inhale and pause for about 10 seconds and then exhale through the other side. If the pause feels good, continue. If it doesn't, shorten the pause. After a few rounds with the short pause, make it a few seconds longer. Very gradually lengthen the pause.

You should find it sweet and absorbing at first. As you hold longer, your feelings will intensify. Let them grow as strong as you are able to witness. At the same time, progress slowly. Never hold so long that the holding on the next side must be shortened. With longer holding times, you can let your hand rest in your lap. You can also change hands as frequently as you need. If your seated position becomes uncomfortable, simply adjust and continue the pranayama.

6) After about 10 rounds of Anuloma Viloma, end the pranayama on an exhale through your left nostril. Then release your hand to your lap and let your breath flow freely.

7) Let your attention drift into your body and feel the effects of what you have done. Many students report feeling energized and peaceful, with their minds expanded. Take at least three to five minutes to explore all the changes in your body, emotions, and mind. When you are ready to move, start slowly. You might feel uncoordinated for a few minutes. Do simple tasks or rest until your mind becomes active again.

Growing into Anuloma Viloma

1) Lengthened holdings. With practice, the breath retentions will lengthen and become more meditative. Some old texts indicate that when your nadis are fully open, you can hold your breath for three hours. They probably meant that it feels like three hours, because you are so absorbed.

2) Visualizations. Visualizations are prescribed in some texts, often based on chakras. Here are several ways to work with this:

- Memorize each chakra's shape and color and visualize it while you hold your breath. For example, spend the first five rounds focusing on the pelvic chakra (muladhara). For the next five rounds, focus on the lower abdominal chakra (svadhisthana) and so on.
- Open your eyes and stare at a drawing of a chakra as you inhale. Then, close your eyes and visualize it inside you as you hold the breath and exhale.
- As you inhale, visualize white light flowing into your nostril, over the top of your head, and down your spine. As you hold, visualize a red light glowing in your lower abdomen. Exhale the red light up your spine, over the top of your head, and out the nostril. This visualization supports balance, with the red light representing the sun (passion) and the white light representing the moon (cooling). The balance and integration comes from the merging of the sun and moon.
- A visualization to support purification would be to imagine that you are inhaling white light flowing in the

nostril and down the spine to your pelvis. Exhale smoky or grey light out the same path in reverse.

3) Mantras and affirmations. The hatha yoga traditions used mantras extensively with meditative pranayamas like Anuloma Viloma. Here are several ways to work with this:
- Repeat the same mantra the entire time you practice Anuloma Viloma. A longer mantra might last for the whole round as you inhale, hold, and exhale. For example, you could use the *Gayatri* mantra:

> Inhale: *Om bhur bhuvah svah*
> Hold: *Tat savitur vareniyam*
> *Bhargo devasya dhimahi*
> Exhale: *Dhiyo yo nah pracodayat*

One translation of the Gayatri mantra is "We meditate on the glory of that Being who has created this universe. May He enlighten our minds."
- A shorter mantra might be repeated three times in each round: once for the inhale, once for the holding, and once for the exhale. An example here would be *Om Namah Shivaya,* meaning "I surrender to that which is benevolent" or "I open myself to you."

Affirmations can be used in the same way as mantras. Here are some examples:
- Recite a long affirmation as you inhale, hold, and exhale. For example, you could use this mantra from the *Ashtavakra Gitra:*

> Inhale: "In me the boundless ocean"
> Hold: "the boat of the universe moves here
> and there, driven by the wind of its own
> inherent nature"

Exhale: "I am not affected."
(Chapter 7, Verse 1)

- A shorter affirmation might be repeated once for the inhale, once for the holding. and once for the exhale. Example: "I am fully alive in this moment."
- Use a different affirmation for each stage of the pranayama. Example: Inhale: "I take in all that is"; hold: "I am strong enough to see my whole self"; exhale: "I let go of everything that isn't me."

Practice Anuloma Viloma until you feel very comfortable with it. It should make you more sensitive and generate an inner strength through challenging you to be present with uncomfortable experience. A traditional way to practice would be to do Dirgha, Ujjayi, and Anuloma Viloma until you feel that this inner strength has been attained. Then, drop Anuloma Viloma, and move to the energy-activating pranayamas (taught in the next section) after Dirgha and Ujjayi.

Another way to practice would be to do Dirgha, Ujjayi, and Anuloma Viloma, then move into the energy-activating pranayamas without dropping Anuloma Viloma. Many modern practitioners choose this option, incorporating Anuloma Viloma in their regular practice.

Traditionally, these practices were done by monks who had teachers to tell them what to practice and when to move on. If you are practicing on your own, you need to decide for yourself how to practice, when you are ready to move onto the next technique, and which sequences to use.

Energy-Activating Pranayamas
Kapalabhati • Bhastrika • Suryabhedana
Murcha • Plavini

Now we move on to a series of energy activating pranayamas, each more intense than the one before: Kapalabhati, Bhastrika, Suryabhedana, Murcha, and Plavini.

Their purpose is to awaken sun energy. **When sun energy floods the nervous system, it dissolves inhibitions and reveals psychological drives beneath the conscious mind. When the practitioner withdraws into the witness state and observes what she feels, the social conditioning is challenged and released.** Old traumas and fears rise to the surface and are integrated.

There are three dynamics found in all the energy-activating pranayamas: 1) vigorous breathing; 2) breath retention; and 3) stimulation of the belly and pelvis. We will examine all three to understand how the energy-activating pranayamas work.

1) Vigorous breathing. All of the energy-activating pranayamas involve vigorous breathing. This affects the gas levels in our blood, specifically, the level of carbon dioxide (CO_2). The amount of oxygen (O_2) in our blood does not change when we do pranayama. There is so much oxygen in the atmosphere (21%) that it easily saturates the hemoglobin in our blood. When we practice pranayama, then, our oxygen levels remain steady.

Carbon dioxide (CO_2), on the other hand, fluctuates with pranayama practice. Carbon dioxide is a waste gas produced by our cells through metabolism. There is very little CO_2 in the atmosphere (less than 0.1%), and it is quickly carried from our lungs and dispersed. When we breathe slowly, we release less CO_2, causing the CO_2 level in the blood to increase. This creates a sense of well-being. When we breathe quickly, we release an excess of CO_2, causing the blood level to reduce slightly. This reduced CO_2 level produces an excitation in the nervous system.

Figure 12. Effects of slow and vigorous breathing

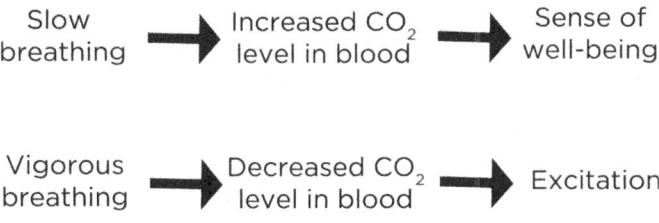

This is the same excitation we feel in our bodies when we have sex, but very different from when we exercise. During exercise, our bodies work to keep the O_2 and CO_2 levels steady. Our breathing adapts to our need for oxygen. Our metabolism increases and we need more O_2 to burn, and therefore create and release more CO_2. We breathe faster to bring in more of the former and eliminate more of the latter. Our breathing continually adjusts to meet our needs and maintain the balance of O_2 and CO_2 in our blood.

In sexual arousal or when a strong emotion arises, the body uses fast breathing to create a CO_2 drop that in sex pushes us over the edge to climax, and with strong emotion pushes us beyond our social conditioning into a fight-or-flight response. When this happens with strong emotions, the mind is usually pulled into the response and we behave without restraint. It feels as if some force came over us and made us do something we normally would not do. The strong emotion is sun energy dissolving our moon, our ahankara, or rational mind.

When a yogi creates this experience in the privacy of the yoga room, the energy is free of emotion and can be very blissful. If it reminds the practitioner of a time in the past where strong emotions arose—a trauma perhaps—it becomes an opportunity for healing, again by witnessing.

This discussion can lead to a few important questions:

Q: Is this process safe when initiated by pranayama?

Yoganand

My experience as a practitioner and teacher has shown me that students can safely grow into the intensity of the sun-activating pranayamas if they do so gradually. Healthy individuals can practice these techniques in the safety of a retreat setting or a cloistered ashram setting and under the supervision of an experienced teacher.

Q: How does one find a safe setting or an experienced teacher?

If you are studying with a yoga teacher that you trust, start by asking them for guidance. If they don't teach these practices themselves, ask them for help in finding a teacher or a retreat where this type of work is led.

Many teachers in the Kripalu and Pranakriya traditions have studied these yoga practices. Yoganand has personally trained thousands of teachers over the past 20 years. You can visit the Pranakriya and Kripalu websites to look into retreats and teachers with the skills and experience to safely guide you.

Q: Why would someone want to dedicate years to such a process?

Yoganand

I believe even a little of this work can be life altering in the growth and healing it can bring. To the extent it is useful to an individual who has the interest, access to a skilled teacher, and the sensitivity to recognize when they have gone too far, the path of activating energy works for profound self-growth.

I do not recommend that everyone practice energy-activating pranayamas. As pranayama practitioners, we should have a thorough understanding of the path as it was developed and practiced in ancient times. From this context, we can discern what level of practice is appropriate for each of us.

We've learned here that vigorous breathing is one dynamic common to all of the energy-activating pranayamas. It increases energy by decreasing the CO_2 level in the blood. Practitioners can safely work with these practices if they grow into them gradually, ideally under the guidance of an experienced teacher.

2) Breath retention. The *Hatha Yoga Pradipika* divides pranayama into three stages, summarized in Figure 13. *Kumbhak*, holding the breath in and out, is one of those three stages and is also the second dynamic common to all of the energy-activating pranayamas.

This is how breath retention works to deepen pranayama. As you begin a breathing exercise, the attention turns inward toward the breath. Suddenly, when you hold in or out, your breath stops. Holding the breath means cutting off the external world and cutting the lifeline, which activates survival fears.

Figure 13. Stages of Breathing

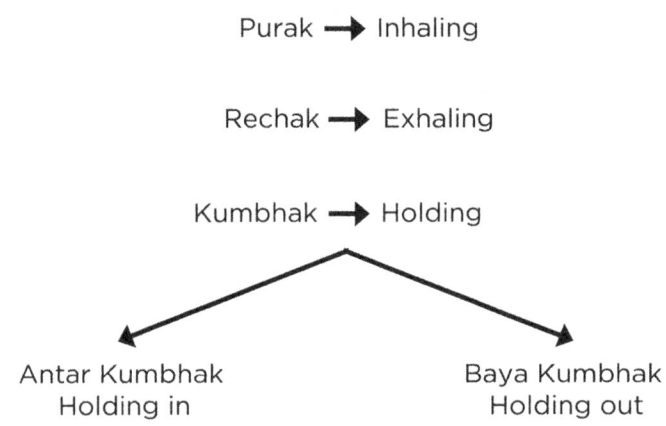

Hatha Yoga Pradipika, Chapter 2, Verses 18 and 71

Normally, when you are afraid, the cause of the fear is in your immediate vicinity. Because of this, you are drawn to respond to the fear. Generating fear through pranayama activates energy, without having any threat in your presence. That means you can watch the fear, since there is no need to respond to it. When the current fear reminds you of past fears, you can watch those, too. Doing so helps to release or integrate the fears, not all at once, but a little bit more each time they are witnessed.

As this process unfolds, a dichotomy emerges between the intensity of the fear and the calm of the witness. This dichotomy creates a churning, which grows more intense the longer the breath is held. There is a point where that churning becomes too strong to witness, and the yogi breathes.

The ancients felt it was a very powerful time when the practitioner was internal, observing the churning and energy activation.

Yoganand

This is why I strongly recommend stopping after each pranayama and taking your awareness inside. When you do a pranayama like Kapalabhati, you stir up energies. When you hold in or out, you elevate your awareness to an exceptionally focused state. When you then release the breath, the intense focus remains, and meditation happens without effort.

The most powerful experience arises from Baya Kumbhak, holding the breath out, because it generates the most sensation. Energy is stirred up and survival-level emotions arise, flooding the abdominal region with feeling. Awareness of this feeling can flow right into sensation, completely absorbing the practitioner.

Antar Kumbhak, holding the breath in, produces less sensation, because it makes us feel more numb. As when we eat a lot of food, sensation inside decreases when the body fills up. Holding in, however, creates a powerful experience in a different way, because it can last much longer than holding out. With certain advanced pranayamas, such as Bhastrika, the holding lasts only for a few seconds, but those few seconds feel incredibly intense. Practicing Bhastrika without the holdings generates a specific energy pattern; practicing Bhastrika with the holdings magnifies the energy pattern tremendously, making it far more powerful.

A healthy adult cannot hold the breath long enough to hurt themselves. Full lungs hold enough oxygen to sustain us for about four minutes. It would take about the same amount of time for carbon dioxide levels to become unhealthy. Yet most people can hold their breath for only about one minute.

In the science of breathing, there is a limit called the "break point." It is the point at which we cannot willfully hold our breath any longer. Scientists used to believe the break point was determined by our bodies' need to consume oxygen or expel carbon dioxide. This is now recognized as untrue. Our current understanding is that the diaphragm muscle was designed to continually move. When it is held still through breath retention, it becomes very uncomfortable and tells the brain that we are in pain. The brain responds, and we have to breathe.

When a yogi works with breath retention after an energy-activating pranayama, she holds her breath and withdraws into her witness. She watches the "need to breathe" energy build. This "need to breathe" energy wants to pull her out of her witness and make her act by releasing her breath and turning her into a "doer." She holds on to the witness as long as she can and, in doing so, her witness grows stronger. When the need for breath becomes stronger than her witness, she releases the breath.

3) Stimulation of the belly and pelvis. We've seen that vigorous breathing and breath retention are common to all of the energy-activating pranayamas. The third element of the energy-activating pranayamas is stimulation of the belly and pelvis.

Stimulating the belly and pelvis happens by repeatedly engaging and releasing muscles in this area of the body. This does two things: 1) it releases tension in the belly and pelvis, enlivening this region of the body; and 2) it activates feelings linked to our primal drives. The two go hand in hand. Let's examine how.

The sun, our passion, lives in the lower abdomen, and the moon, our rational self, lives in the crown of the head. The moon fears the sun and builds a wall between itself and the sun, a wall between reason and passion. If you're at work and something makes you really angry, you might want to run away, attack, or behave in an otherwise unrestrained way. That is sun energy rising up. The moon is your ego mind or restraint, and it steers you away from the primal behavior.

Think of all the times in a day when you control yourself: setting your alarm to wake up at a certain time, deciding how much to eat for breakfast, driving to avoid speeding tickets, taking a specific path to your desk to avoid people who trigger you. The moon helps you maneuver through the whole day in a controlled manner. It wants you to be 100 percent rational.

If we didn't have this restraint, we wouldn't have a civil society, so the control of the moon is needed. But, when we're so restrained all the time, we need a release by the end of the day or the end of the week. So we go out to a bar and drink too much, snack too much in the evening, or play violent video games.

Being so restrained also causes us to build an armor in the belly that becomes chronic, and this cuts us off from a wealth of vitality and radiance. **The ancient yogis wanted to go into a private place and be primal in order to safely reclaim the aliveness of their sun energy.**

Releasing tension in the belly and pelvis breaks down the wall between the moon and the sun. It unleashes sun energy. **This tension is released both through the physical process of contracting and relaxing the muscles in the vigorous pranayamas and the energetic process of flooding the body with energy so the ego dissolves.** Ancient yogis believed that tension in the body was connected to ego rigidity. When the ego dissolves, physical tension melts.

Stimulating the belly and pelvis can activate primal experiences such as anger, fear, and sexual energy. When they are witnessed and their labels are removed, they become "yoga fire" or pure ecstasy. This increases the yogi's energy and aliveness.

Yogis would say that the afterglow and openness we feel after sex is partially because of the release of tension in the belly and the dissolving of the ego in the orgasm experience. Without being sexual, pranayama can generate a similar openness and glow.

In the sexual experience, the belly and pelvis are flooded with energy and move spontaneously. In a vigorous pranayama experience, there is a movement in this part of the body that is completely non-sexual but that is the same movement our belly and pelvis make in sex. The effect on the body is similar. There should not be genital stimulation in pranayama, but the belly can feel similar to sex during and after a vigorous pranayama.

Thus, the energy-activating pranayamas release physical tension and unleash the primal self, which leads to greater wholeness, as we reclaim the animal part of the self. They also create heightened bliss, as we convert our primal energy into pure energy.

Safety Awarenesses

In addition to the safety awarenesses discussed at the start of this chapter, the following conditions are contraindications for energy-activating pranayamas: uncontrolled high blood pressure; recent surgery; neck, shoulder, or spinal injuries; hernias; colitis; ulcers; heart problems; and mental or emotional instability. Energy-activating pranayamas are not recommended during pregnancy.

You might want to avoid these vigorous pranayamas if you have inflammation of the sinuses or throat, indigestion, or other abdominal discomfort. If excess mucus from a cold makes the pranayama difficult, do not strain. If you have a cold or flu and are contagious, do not practice near others to avoid spreading your illness. If you find your ears popping a lot, you might need to hydrate. If drinking water doesn't help, you should back off or stop the pranayama.

Some contemporary writings on pranayama warn that practitioners can pass out and their fingernails can turn blue from some of the energy-activating pranayamas included in this section. Even in working with thousands of students over several decades, Yoganand has never seen this.

Kapalabhati Pranayama: Skull-Polishing Breath

The first energy-activating pranayama is Kapalabhati. Before we dive into Kapalabhati, let's step back to clarify a seeming discrepancy. The hatha yoga texts clearly define Kapalabhati as a kriya (a cleansing technique), not a pranayama (a breathing technique). This can be confusing since Kapalabhati is a breathing exercise, making it seem like a pranayama, and Kapalabhati is similar to Bhastrika, another energy-activating technique that *is* called a pranayama.

So why, then, is it considered a kriya in the texts? Kapalabhati's categorization as a kriya has more to do with its intention than its technique. Remember that the purpose of a kriya is to cleanse. You can see in the following passage that the texts focus on Kapalabhati's cleansing effects of reducing mucus and overcoming the sluggishness of the kapha constitution (The Ayurvedic equivalent of an endomorphic body).

> *The process of releasing and drawing in breath quickly like a bellows is well known as Kapalabhati. This Kriya is the remover of the ailments of Kapha. If one does Pranayama after the excess weight is lost through the six actions, he will achieve success without difficulty.* (Hatha Yoga Pradipika, Chapter 2, Verses 35–36)

Most likely, Kapalabhati was taught to the student first with an emphasis on purification. When the student was ready for energy activation, the teacher taught Bhastrika, building on the work the student did with

Kapalabhati. In other words, Kapalabhati grew to become Bhastrika.

For our purposes, we are focusing on the energy activation of Kapalabhati more than its cleansing abilities. So we will treat Kapalabhati as the first of the energy-activating pranayamas.

Kapalabhati Technique

Kapalabhati is a series of strong exhalations through the nose followed by passive inhalations, also through the nose. It is usually practiced in a seated position with the waist lengthened. This will focus the epicenter of the contraction in the solar plexus. The pelvis and ribs are held still so that only the belly moves.

Some traditions teach that these exhalations should be done quickly and shallowly. Our focus is on strong exhalations. Speed is determined by the student's ability to relax the belly after each exhale and allow the passive inhale.

Kapalabhati will tend to be slow for beginning students (about one breath every two seconds) and much faster for experienced students (two to three breaths per second). A round of Kapalabhati can be anywhere from 20 exhalations up to several hundred. Do not practice past the point where your abdominal muscles are too tired to hold your pelvis and ribs still.

The benefits of Kapalabhati are that it frees tension in the belly, heightens energy by decreasing CO_2, creates a sense of increased aliveness, dilates nasal passages and clears mucus from them, exchanges the air in the lungs rapidly, and strengthens the transverse and oblique abdominal muscles.

Kapalabhati Preliminary Exercise

1) Sit straight and tall on a cushion or in a chair.

2) Bring one palm to rest on your solar plexus and hold the other palm a few inches away from your mouth.

3) Imagine that you have a votive candle in your raised hand. Take a deep breath and with a quick, sharp exhale, blow out your candle. Repeat this exhale several times.

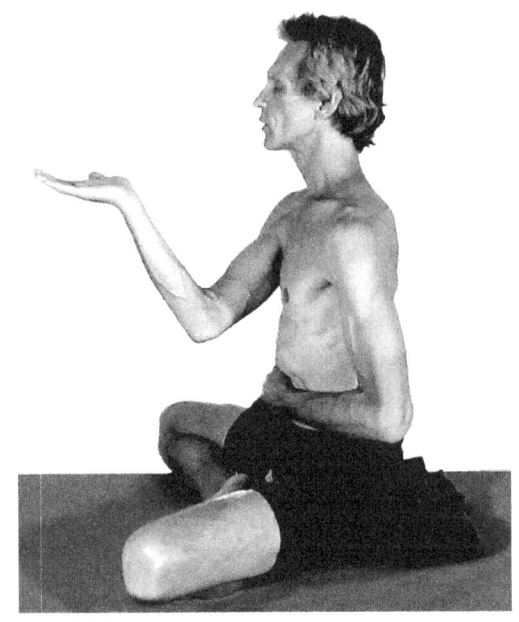

Blowing out an imaginary candle to create a quick, sharp exhale

4) Notice that your belly contracts each time you blow. Notice also that you do not have to consciously inhale. It happens automatically when you relax your belly in between exhalations.

5) Now imagine you want to blow out the imaginary candle with your nose. Do this softly the first couple of times. If you feel pressure or popping in your ears, make your exhalations gentler. Again, notice that the inhalation happens automatically upon relaxing your belly.

6) Let go of the image of the candle and hold both hands against your belly. Exhale strongly through your mouth. Let your belly relax for a passive inhale. After the inhale, exhale again, and repeat.

7) After 20 cycles of this breathing pattern, let your breathing return to normal. Sit quietly and feel. You might feel very energized, especially in your belly. You might also feel spacey, as if your mind has expanded.

If you feel any of the symptoms described in the list of safety awarenesses, stop the exercise and take slow, deep breaths. Lie down if you feel dizzy.

Practicing Kapalabhati Pranayama

1) Sit comfortably in a cross-legged position, kneeling, or on a chair, as described in Chapter 5. Wobble a little side to side and back to front to make sure your seat provides adequate and balanced support. If your seat does not support you properly, your abdominal muscles will work harder and be less available for breathing.

2) Bring your body to stillness. Feel your spine and lengthen it as much as you can by pulling your tailbone down and the top of your neck up. Pull your shoulders forward and up, and then back and down. Pull your shoulder blades in toward your spine and down toward your sacrum, but keep your spine long.

With your spine elongated you will feel the Kapalabhati contractions in your solar plexus. To be sure the contractions are happening in the solar plexus, place your hand there to feel the movement. If your spine is not elongated, you might feel the contraction lower in your abdomen. When the contraction is strongest in your solar plexus, the contractions will cause an upward pull on your muscles that is considered ideal for activating sun energy.

3) Practice Dirgha and Ujjayi pranayamas for several minutes to warm up your body and mind.

4) Begin Kapalabhati breathing with a strong exhalation through your nose. Then relax your belly, allowing it to return to its resting position. This will accompany an inhalation that you might not feel. As soon as you feel that your belly has relaxed, exhale strongly again. As you practice, do not lean forward or round your back.

Strong exhale through the nose

Relaxing the belly to resting position
for a passive inhale through the nose

5) Continue until your belly feels tired. For beginners, 20 expulsions is a good starting point. With practice, a round of Kapalabhati can grow up to several hundred expulsions.

6) When you are ready to stop this round of Kapalabhati, take an active, deep inhalation and release it slowly. Take a second deep breath, and then breathe normally. Let your attention drift into your body, and feel the effects. Take at least three to five minutes to explore all the changes to your body, emotions, and mind.

Each round of Kapalabhati potentially generates more energy inside. The energy grows as much as we allow it to grow. There is a point at which we tighten up and stop letting energy come in. As long as we allow it to do so, Kapalabhati will raise energy.

In order to enliven the abdominal region, Kapalabhati must be done correctly. The slow, strong exhalations contract the rectus abdominis muscle and, to some extent, the transverse abdominis muscles. The passive inhalation happens when those muscles relax. The goal is to repeatedly take the belly from engaged to completely relaxed. When practitioners start out, it takes a few seconds to relax after each contraction, because the belly has not learned to be responsive. Beginners tend to inhale willfully, but we want a willful breath out and a passive breath in.

Yoganand

One of my hobbies is kung fu. When I am in the ring and somebody throws a side kick toward my belly, it tightens up to repel the kick. Then it softens again. It can be as tight as it needs to be, but it responds to the situation, rather than staying tight all the time.

If I go to see my auto mechanic, my armor engages as he tells me how much the repairs will cost. When I leave, the armor disappears.

When I eat a big meal, my stomach asks the muscles to give them some space. The belly softens so that the food can move.

This is what we mean by a responsive belly. It knows how to engage just the right amount for each situation. Then it knows how to relax when the engagement is no longer needed.

After Kapalabhati, the belly should feel tired and more open. When the belly muscles relax, a layer of armor could potentially melt away. It is not unusual to feel vulnerable after a round of Kapalabhati, as if something is moving inside. That is perfectly okay, because we are breaking open and dissolving armor in the belly. Without that, we might be turning over the air in the lungs and cleaning out the nasal passages, but we are missing a deep benefit of the practice—increased opening and aliveness.

Growing into Kapalabhati

The exercise above is basic Kapalabhati. Once you are extremely comfortable with it, you might wish to explore the following enhancements. Do not try them until basic Kapalabhati feels effortless.

Basic Kapalabhati gives us the vigorous breathing that lowers carbon dioxide and the abdominal movement that activates primal sun energy. **Adding breath retention gives us Kapalabhati in full effect, by activating the primal emotion of fear.** The breath retention techniques presented here should only be practiced with objectivity and discrimination.

1) External breath retention. Practice Kapalabhati until you are tired. Then, inhale deeply through your nose and exhale fully through your mouth. Rounding your back can help you achieve the fullest exhale. Hold your breath out and lengthen your torso upward. Holding your breath out can make your abdomen feel empty. Elongating upward through your torso pulls that emptiness down toward your pelvis.

As you hold out, shift your mind into an observing mode. Look down into the emptiness in your belly and watch it. When the sun energy is activated, it will appear as the need for breath. Witness the rising need for as long as you can. When the need becomes stronger than your witness, release the holding and let your breath flow freely. Stay attuned to your inner experience.

When you are comfortable with holding your breath out, you can add *Mulabandha* mudra to the holding (see Chapter 7).

You can modify this external breath retention by taking two or three slow, deep breaths before exhaling to hold out. The modified sequence would be: Kapalabhati, 2-3 deep breaths, external holding.

2) External, then internal breath retention. This technique builds on the external breath retention we just learned.

Practice Kapalabhati, then hold your breath out until the need for breath is strong, as described above. Next, inhale sharply and hold your breath in. As you hold in, stay long through your waist and neck. Focus your attention on your third-eye point (between and above your eyebrows), and watch the rising need for breath. You might notice that focusing on your third eye pulls your attention up, while the need for breath pulls your awareness down. Just watch. When the need becomes stronger than your witness, release the holding and let your breath flow freely. Stay attuned to your inner experience.

Hold only as long as you can keep your mind as the open and present witness. If you notice yourself shutting down to hold longer, you've gone too far and will not receive the full benefits of the practice. Do not shut down in order to hold.

3) Internal, then external breath retention. Practice this breath retention sequence only if you are comfortable with the first two. This sequence of internal, then external breath retention is described in the *Hatha Yoga Pradipika* (Chapter 2, Verse 45–46) for advanced students who have the presence, time, and environment to allow their minds to expand and then take a while to become more focused again.

After a round of Kapalabhati, inhale fully, and hold in with your attention on your third eye. When the need is too strong to witness, exhale through your mouth and hold out. Elongate, and focus on the emptiness in your abdomen. When the need becomes stronger than your witness, release the holding and let your breath flow freely. Stay attuned to your inner experience.

If you practice this sequence of breath retentions, we recommend sitting in meditation afterward for at least 10 minutes to help yourself to ground.

4) Alternate-Nostril Kapalabhati. The first three enhancements for Kapalabhati involve breath retention *after* your round of expulsions. The next two techniques are variations *within* the round of Kapalabhati itself.

In this variation, you alternate nostrils for the exhalations. The inhalations still happen spontaneously through both nostrils, just like basic Kapalabhati.

Use your thumb to block your right nostril, exhale strongly through the left, then release the right nostril for the passive inhale. Then use your finger to block the left nostril, exhale strongly through the right, then release the left nostril for the passive inhale. Continue alternating between nostrils in this way. A common mistake is exhaling and inhaling through one nostril, then switching sides. Make sure you are releasing the nostrils for the passive inhalations.

When practicing this pranayama, be aware that you are not blocking both nostrils at the same time. Having both nostrils open for the inhale lets it happen faster, so you don't have to slow your pranayama down. It is also safer for your ears if you make sure one or both nostrils are fully open at all times. That is, be careful not to partially block one nostril as you switch to the other.

The traditional hand position for this practice is *Vishnu* mudra and is illustrated below. Any other hand position that works for you is acceptable, and you can use either your left or right hand.

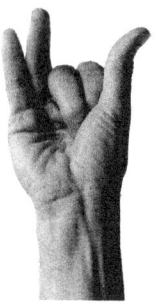

Vishnu mudra

Alternate-Nostril Kapalabhati with Vishnu mudra

Alternate-Nostril Kapalabhati requires less effort than the basic technique, because exhaling through one nostril makes the hole smaller. The smaller hole allows the exhaling muscles to easily push against the air in the lungs, which means you can do more expulsions before becoming tired.

You can feel the difference in exertion if you try a few Kapalabhati exhales through your open mouth, then a few exhales through both nostrils, then one nostril. The mouth is the largest opening, which makes Kapalabhati the most tiring because the muscles have little to push against. Exhaling through both nostrils is a bit easier, and through one nostril easiest of all.

A benefit of Alternate-Nostril Kapalabhati is that the blast is stronger through each nostril, because the air that was going through both is now channeled through only one. This leads to enhanced physical cleansing.

You may practice any breath retention sequence after each round of Alternate-Nostril Kapalabhati.

5) Single-Nostril Kapalabhati. A more advanced version involves Kapalabhati through only one nostril at a time. For Single-Nostril Kapalabhati, block one nostril with your thumb or finger and practice Kapalabhati through the other nostril. Using only one nostril for the exhalation and inhalation requires that you do the Kapalabhati slower than normal.

This is more advanced than Alternate-Nostril Kapalabhati because your belly needs to be very responsive for the air to flow freely. If the belly is not responsive, it will take too long to inhale and will feel uncomfortable. Again, this means it is very important to practice a strong contraction for the exhale, then totally let go for the passive inhale.

After practicing this version, you might feel that the side of your body that you breathed through is more alive or more energized than the other. As with Alternate-Nostril Kapalabhati, a benefit of Single-Nostril Kapalabhati is that the blast is stronger through the nostril, which leads to better physical cleansing of mucus from the nasal passages. Always practice a second round to balance the sides. Again, you may practice any breath retention sequence after each round.

Bhastrika Pranayama: Bellows Breath

Bhastrika is a vigorous pranayama that generates more energy than Kapalabhati. New students can feel uncomfortable with the amount of energy aroused by Bhastrika. If the student can relax into the energy, it can be blissful. If they fight it, the pranayama becomes uncomfortable. They might experience dizziness, nausea, or anxiety. Because of this, Bhastrika is not appropriate for everyone. If you find Bhastrika uncomfortable in any way, do not continue practice.

Bhastrika Technique

Let's look at the *Hatha Yoga Pradipika*'s teaching on Bhastrika:

> *Both clean feet should be placed on the thighs. This posture is Padmasana (lotus posture) and is the destroyer of all sins.* (Chapter 2, Verse 59)

The above verse indicates that someone practicing Bhastrika should be an experienced yogi. Because of the warm climate in India, most people wear sandals without socks, so their feet become calloused and often have deep cracks. Clean feet indicate the person is a long-time yogi living a quiet internal life, not traveling around and weathering their feet. The ability to sit in Lotus posture (Padmasana) indicates this is an experienced student who has been practicing for some time.

The next verse states:

The wise Sadhaka should hold his abdomen and head erect. Having closed the mouth, he should strongly exhale so that the heart, throat, and head are filled with sound. Then quickly draw in the air to fill the chest. Thus, the Sadhaka should repeatedly release out and draw in. Just as a blacksmith works a bellows quickly so the Sadhaka should work the Prana with good judgment. (Chapter 2, Verses 60–62)

Whereas Kapalabhati is a series of strong exhalations followed by passive inhalations, Bhastrika consists of strong exhalations *and* strong inhalations. The exhalations and inhalations should be of equal intensity and speed. If one is consistently stronger or faster than the other, the student can become dizzy quickly.

The student should start out slow, generate a steady rhythm, and then gradually speed up. If the student can surrender into the practice, the energy will take over and the body will find its own speed and intensity.

To "work the Prana with good judgment" means keeping the mind focused on the practice, feeling the rhythm, and letting the body set the pace, without feeling competitive or fearful. It also means remaining connected to how the body feels, allowing the body to determine when to stop. In a sexual experience, the body moves at a speed that is just right, without any help from the mind, and that free movement through the nervous system turns into orgasm. In this same way, the energy of Bhastrika should be allowed to take over.

> *When fatigue appears in the body, inhale through the Surya Nadi (right nostril) in such a way that the abdomen becomes filled with air. Using the thumb, ring, and little fingers, he should firmly hold his nose. After having systematically held this Kumbhaka, he should exhale through the Ida Nadi (left nostril).* (Verses 64–65)

The classical instruction is to hold internal breath retention after completing the vigorous inhalations and exhalations. We encourage students to do the following: 1) first practice without any breath retention; 2) progress to holding the breath out, then holding the breath in; and 3) when comfortable with the above retention sequence, move to holding the breath in first, then exhaling to hold the breath out. We will cover these retention sequences further in the instruction section for Bhastrika.

The text says to inhale through *surya nadi* (right nostril) and exhale through *ida nadi* (left nostril). Our experience has shown that it does not matter which nostril you use, and we encourage students to inhale and exhale through both nostrils at the same time. This is safer than trying to remember which nostril to use when you are in the energetic experience of Bhastrika.

> *This Kumbhaka named Bhastrika is the killer of the diseases of Kapha, Vata, and Pitta. It increases desirable heat inside the body and arouses Kundalini (the strongest form of sun energy) quickly. It is beneficial and brings comfort. It removes the mucus that blocks the mouth of the Brahma Nadi. It perfectly penetrates the three Granthis of the body and should be given special attention.* (Chapter 2, Verse 65-7)

When the wave of sun energy subsides after practicing Bhastrika, there should be profound balance in the body and mind. All the thoughts, fears, belief systems, and conditioning that distort the body with tension and the mind with emotion should be temporarily wiped away. This is the balancing of the Ayurvedic energies kapha, vata, and pitta.

The "desirable heat" is the sun burning while the mind remains detached, so the mind observes the burning sun, but is not driven by its heat. The kundalini is a reference to awakening animal energy, which again is witnessed, not pulling us into action. The brahma nadi is the mythical doorway to liberation. It is sushumna, the central channel in the body in which the sun (apana) and moon (ahankara) disappear.

The three granthis are three knots that bind the soul to the body. Brahma granthi is the knot created by our needs and animal drives, and the tangle of karma that results when we try to meet them. Vishnu granthi involves our relationship to the world and the social drives that pull us into relationship. Rudra granthi is about our relationship with God and all the existential questions that can cause insecurity and fear. The above verse tells us that Bhastrika untangles these three knots.

The benefits of Bhastrika are the same as the benefits of Kapalabhati, only stronger. Bhastrika frees tension in the belly, heightens energy by decreasing CO_2, creates a sense of well-being, dilates nasal passages, rapidly exchanges the air in the lungs, and strengthens the transverse and oblique abdominal muscles.

Practicing Bhastrika Pranayama

1) Sit comfortably in a cross-legged position or kneeling, as described in Chapter 5. Creating a stable foundation in

Bhastrika is very important. Sitting in a chair is not recommended. Wobble a little side to side and back to front to make sure your seat provides adequate and balanced support. If your seat does not support you properly, your abdominal muscles will have to work harder and will be less available for breathing.

2) Bring your body to stillness. Feel your spine, and lengthen it as much as you can by pulling your tailbone down and the top of your neck up. Pull your shoulders forward and up, and then back and down. Pull your shoulder blades in toward your spine and down toward your sacrum, but keep your spine long.

3) Practice Dirgha and Ujjayi pranayamas for several minutes to warm up your body and mind.

4) Begin Bhastrika breathing with a strong exhale through your nose. Do not lean forward or drop your chest. Immediately inhale as strongly as you exhaled. Repeat strong exhales and inhales at a steady pace.

5) If you feel comfortable with Bhastrika, let your body find its own pace. It might slow down or speed up. Keep your attention focused on strong inhales and exhales, making sure they are equal in speed and intensity.

6) Continue until your belly feels tired, about 20 to 30 expulsions. If you feel lightheaded or experience any discomfort, stop immediately.

7) When you are ready to stop this round of Bhastrika, take a full breath in and release it slowly. Breathe normally for about three minutes, until you feel calm again. Then do a second round of Bhastrika. When you are finished, return to

your natural breath, and let your attention drift into your body and feel the effects. Take at least three to five minutes to explore all the changes in your body, emotions, and mind.

Growing into Bhastrika

The instructions above are for the basic Bhastrika technique. Once you are extremely comfortable with the basic technique, you might wish to explore the following enhancements. Do not try them until basic Bhastrika feels effortless.

1) Breath retention. As with Kapalabhati, you can end Bhastrika with a breath retention sequence. If you have found a sequence that you like for Kapalabhati, practice it here.

We suggest beginning by holding the breath out, then holding the breath in. When you are comfortable with the above retention sequence, move to holding the breath in first, then exhaling to hold the breath out.

The breath retention sequence will be more powerful if you add affirmations or visualizations to your practice. Use any that feel good to you. Here is an example of a visualization: While inhaling, visualize feeding a fire in your belly that is blazing brightly like the sun. After your retention, exhale, and imagine you are pulling the sun energy up to the realm of the moon as the breath comes up and out of your body.

Here is an example of an affirmation: When you hold your breath out, you might imagine you are diving into your past, which is stored in your belly and pelvis: "I dive into my past and witness." When you hold in, you might affirm that you are rising up into your spiritual self or rising up to your highest potential: "I rise up into my higher self." Again, only do this if it helps you dive deeper into your practice.

2) Arm movement. You can add an arm movement to Bhastrika to enhance the inhalations and exhalations. First, prepare for Bhastrika by finding your seated position. Then make loose fists with your hands and hold them up in front of your shoulders. As you inhale, shoot your hands high into the air and open your fingers wide. Allow your ribs to open wide and your back to arch slightly. As you exhale, pull your hands back to your shoulders and close them to make fists, rounding your back slightly.

Continue raising and lowering your hands with each inhale and exhale. Remember, the arm movements are intended to enhance the breath, so make sure the movement is coordinated with the breath. They need to support each other and work together.

Round and arch your back only within a comfortable range that comes naturally as you reach the arms up and down. Keep your head as an extension of your spine, and do not drop it back when you inhale.

This variation of Bhastrika opens the lungs and belly a little more than the basic version. Practice it only after you are comfortable with basic Bhastrika and can do so without compromising your body's safety.

Enhancing Bhastrika by reaching hands high into the air during strong inhalations

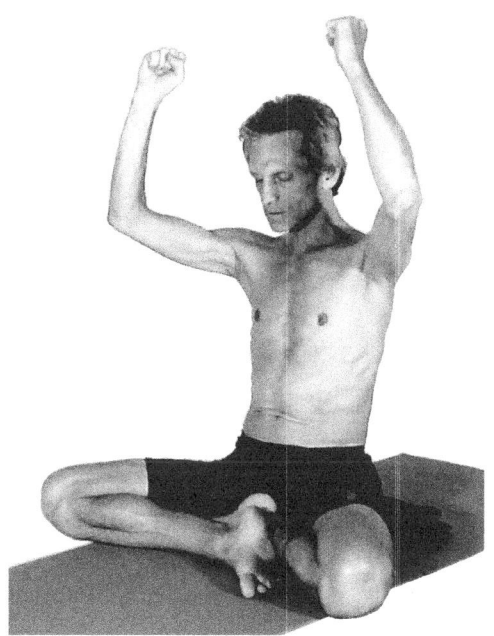
Pulling hands back to the shoulders on strong exhalations

3) Torso movement. Another variation of Bhastrika, known as "Howling Wolf," adds a torso movement to the practice.

Prepare for Bhastrika by finding a stable seated position, kneeling or sitting cross-legged. Lean forward and place your palms on the floor in front of you. Inhale and straighten your arms, lifting your head and slightly arching your back. Exhale and bend your elbows, bringing your forehead close to the floor as you round your back. Continue raising and lowering your body with each inhalation and exhalation. Keep your palms connected with the floor at all times to increase stability and prevent yourself from bumping your head on the floor.

Lifting the torso helps draw the breath in. Folding forward helps to press the breath out. With both versions of Bhastrika, the movement needs to enhance the breath; if it fails to do so, the movement is not worth doing.

Again, make sure the movement is well coordinated with the breath. Only round and arch your back within a comfortable range that comes naturally as you lift and lower your torso. Keep your head as an extension of your spine, and do not drop it back when you inhale.

This variation of Bhastrika opens the lungs and back a bit more than the basic version. Practice it only after you are comfortable with the basic version and can do so without compromising your body's safety. You can also practice this version kneeling, which is a good option for beginners, since it is very stable.

Enhancing Bhastrika by lifting the torso
on strong inhalations

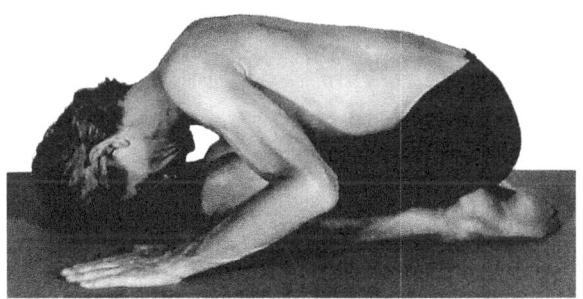

Lowering forehead to the floor on strong exhalations

Bhastrika is one of the most powerful techniques for safely breaking down the wall between the sun (apana or passionate, animal self) and the moon (ahankara or controlled, rational self). This is because it is extremely effective for releasing tensions and enlivening the abdomen. As you explore it, stay connected to how it feels for you and adjust in any way that supports your exploration.

Suryabhedana Pranayama: Sun Piercing Breath

The sun-activating pranayamas were traditionally practiced by students in their late twenties and thirties, at the height of their physical strength, who had begun doing pranayama in their teens or earlier. By this time, they had a strong base of practice and had become comfortable with sun energy. In addition, they had spent some of their formative years practicing yoga and a sattvic (pure) lifestyle, which meant they avoided many of the traumas and wounds that many adults in our culture must carry.

Students with this background would have a different experience with the pranayamas than we would. They would do the work with them and move on, transitioning to a more meditative practice as they moved into their forties and beyond. Those without this kind of background or who have aged beyond the time when they were strongest should be very cautious with sun-activating pranayamas.

For most modern practitioners, Kapalabhati and Bhastrika are all we need to generate an abundance of sun energy. Ancient yogis sometimes chose to go farther into sun activation than would be appropriate for us today. They were not aware of many of the health factors we now know, and their renunciate lifestyles allowed them to spend hours or days in expanded states or integrating past experiences.

We do not recommend the next three pranayamas (Suryabhedana, Murcha, and Plavini) for modern practitioners. We are including the trajectory of their practice here for context, history, and understanding.

"Suryabhedana" literally means "sun piercing" and is a clear reference to the intended effect, which we will examine here.

In the *Hatha Yoga Pradipika*, it is described as follows:

> *After being seated in a convenient and comfortable Asana, the Yogi should gradually draw in the Prana from outside inhaling through the right Nadi. From the hair to the tips of the fingers he should restrain it. Then he should release out through the left Nadi. The excellent Suryabhedana Kumbhaka is the purifier of the head and the brain and is the remover of all ailments caused by Vata and worms. This should be repeatedly practiced.* (Chapter 2, Verses 48–50)

The phrase "from the hair to the tips of the fingers" does not make sense to modern practitioners, so it is often ignored. What remains is a variation of Anuloma Viloma, where the air is always drawn in through the right nostril and released through the left.

The intended technique is explained a little more clearly in the *Gheranda Samhita*:

> *Inspire with all your strength through the sun nadi. Restrain this air with the greatest care while performing Jalandhara Sudra (throat lock). Maintain the kumbhaka as long as perspiration does not burst out from the tips of the nails and the roots of the hair.* (Chapter 5, Verses 58–59)

Describing an advanced variation of Suryabhedana where the pranayama is done in a posture, the *Hatha Yoga Pradipika* states:

> ...after holding until the presence of death is felt the Yogi should release the air. (Chapter 3, Verse 28)

What is indicated in these verses is to inhale through your right nostril until you are full. Hold until you feel you are losing consciousness, and then exhale. When this is practiced there is often a wave of emotion after the exhale. We feel as if we have survived a great danger. We are both very vulnerable and very joyful. The yogis believed that this wave of sun energy stirs us all the way down to the core.

"Piercing the sun" means piercing the wall that the moon (rational self) builds between itself and the sun (passionate self). That wave of fight-or-flight energy is sun energy. If it is witnessed, it is "yoga fire" or pure exhilaration.

Often Suryabhedana was practiced after Kapalabhati or Bhastrika for an extra energy surge. Again, we do not recommend it, but want you to understand the original practices.

Murcha Pranayama: Swooning Breath

"Murcha" means to swoon or pass out. It is described as follows.

> The Kumbhaka named the "Chitta (mind) swoon" is the giver of happiness. It is practiced at the end of drawing in with completely steady Jalandhara bandha (throat lock)

> *and then by gradually releasing out.* (*Hatha Yoga Pradipika*, Chapter 2, Verse 69)

Murcha is practiced by inhaling completely and then holding internal breath retention with the throat lock. When the yogi feels that he can't hold any longer, he lets a little air slip out. Then he finds he can hold for a long time. Again, when he must breathe, he lets a little air slip out. He repeats this as many times as he can, until just before passing out.

Murcha is even stronger than Suryabhedana, which is stronger than Bhastrika. Often Murcha would be part of the breath retention sequence that followed Bhastrika or Kapalabhati. Again, we do not feel confident that Murcha is safe, so we do not suggest you try it.

Plavini Pranayama: Floating Breath

With Plavini pranayama we make a change in our trajectory. Instead of creating urgency through more intense breath retentions, the yogi
generates nausea and practices watching it.

Plavini is not well described in the hatha yoga texts. Very few commentators, including Swami Kripalu, have added much of substance. A basic description from the *Hatha Yoga Pradipika* is below.

> *The Yogi with his abdomen completely filled with air floats on the surface of deep water happily like a lotus leaf.* (Chapter 2, Verse 70)

The traditional description of the practice is to inhale repeatedly with your mouth open. When you feel that your mouth is full of air, you swallow some of the air. This can be done with slow deep breathing but can also be done with Kapalabhati or Bhastrika. Eventually your belly feels bloated and you feel nauseous. If you witness the nausea, it feels like an intoxication—similar to drinking alcohol to the point where you are almost sick, and you oscillate from feeling really good to feeling dizzy or nauseous. In this vulnerable state, some yogis felt you could learn things about yourself that you couldn't learn in a normal state.

There are stories of yogis practicing Plavini until the belly was full of air, then floating on water. This may be where the phrase "floating like a lotus leaf" originates. It could also be a reference to the floating feeling and mind-expansion that Plavini causes.

In this section, we've looked at five traditional pranayamas used to awaken sun energy: Kapalabhati, Bhastrika, Murcha and Plavini. Two of these, Kapalabhati and Bhastrika, are appropriate for modern practitioners. We learned that by watching the sun energy as an objective witness, the yogi can heal, integrate and become more whole. In the next section, we'll look at more ways to work with sun energy by practicing pranayamas designed to channel energy.

Pranayamas for Channeling Energy
Ujjayi • Shitali • Sitkari • Bhramari

Once the yogi has activated an appropriate amount of energy, the final stage of pranayama is to channel the energy. You can think of this as channeling sun energy into sushumna, the central channel in the body. When this happens, both the sun (primal drives) and the moon (rational mind) dissolve, so there is only eternal presence.

Sun-activating pranayamas tend to be intense to practice, involving vigorous movement and/or breath retention. **Energy-channeling pranayamas tend to be meditative, taking the energized body and mind and leading them to a place of peaceful harmony.** They do this not by taking the energy away, but by helping us integrate it and relax into it.

Energy-channeling pranayamas can be practiced independently, in which case they usually have a meditative or calming effect. This is apparent with our first energy-channeling pranayama, Ujjayi. We first covered Ujjayi as a warm-up pranayama. Practiced at the beginning of a pranayama session, usually combined with Dirgha pranayama, Ujjayi calms the restless mind and helps to generate introversion and body awareness. In this section, we will look at how Ujjayi works as an energy-channeling pranayama.

Safety Awarenesses

The energy-channeling pranayamas are usually safe for anyone to practice unless there is respiratory infection or inflammation. In that case, they may cause dizziness or vertigo. If you don't feel good on a particular day, don't practice them.

Ujjayi Pranayama: Victorious Breath

Energy-activating pranayamas create an excitation in the body and an expansion of the mind. When the mind is in this expanded state, the Ujjayi sound, taught in the warm-up section of this chapter, pulls the mind into deep concentration.

When the mind is expanded by the sun-activating pranayamas, it loses its ability to grasp things. We feel very clear inside, but it's almost impossible to focus on a task. Spending time in this state gives us rest from the pressures of daily life, but it becomes a dead end. We would drift aimlessly if there weren't something to take us farther.

The hatha yoga texts frequently use the term "nada" in reference to meditation and pranayama. Nada means "flow of sweetness." It is usually associated with music or sound but it could be any flow of sweet sensation or consciousness. Here is an example of a reference in the *Hatha Yoga Pradipika*:

> *Shri Guru Nathaji (the Hindu god Shiva) only knows the ever-expanding and unique bliss occurring in the hearts of Yogis through the constant practice of Samadhi (dissolving the thinking mind into the witness), along with absorption in Nada (sweet internal flow). A Tapasvi Muni (silent ascetic) closes the ears with both hands and listens to the spontaneous Nada. Let him keep his mind unshakable until complete steadiness and composure are attained.* (Chapter 4, Verses 81–82)

Nada is the sweetness of pure existence, where there is no separate self. Nada is often associated with *laya* in the old texts. Laya means "to dissolve" and is a reference to the mind (ego and thinking self) dissolving into pure consciousness. Laya is a goal of hatha yoga and is sometimes emphasized and expanded to become Laya Yoga. Laya is said to be a byproduct of nada, so the dissolving that happens in meditation (laya) depends upon the flow of pure existence where there is no separation.

Here, the *Hatha Yoga Pradipika* describes this relationship between laya and nada:

> *The master of the organs of action and sense is the mind and the master of the mind is the Prana. The master of the Prana is Laya and this Laya depends on the divine Nada.* (Chapter 4, Verses 28–29)

After practicing the sun-activating pranayamas, the student begins to make the Ujjayi sound. At first, the sound might feel like a smoke screen, separating us from objects and people we care about and think about. This can generate resistance, as we begin to fear that the sound is swallowing us and the external objects are moving farther away. **If we can release resistance and temporarily let go of the external objects, the sound becomes mysterious and absorbing** (nada). It's all we experience, and that is the moon (ahankara or thinking self) dissolving so that we can feel bliss (laya).

Yoganand

Sometimes I wake up in the night and hear the muffled sound of the refrigerator running down the hall. Because I am half asleep, I think I hear jumbled voices in the sound, like an FM radio just out of tune. In that expanded state, I think that, if I just focused a little harder, I could understand what they are saying.

This is how Ujjayi works as an energy-channeling pranayama. You hear a sweet tone in the Ujjayi sound (nada) and the more you try to listen, the deeper you go. Eventually you become the hearer, the hearing, and the space holding it all. Then, having served its purpose, the Ujjayi sound fades away. The sun and moon disappear, and laya, or a sense of eternal meditative presence, remains.

Shitali and Sitkari Pranayamas: Cooling Breaths

The next two pranayamas for channeling energy are Shitali and Sitkari. These two techniques create the same effect, but in different ways. The main difference is that Shitali can only be practiced by students who can curl their tongues, whereas Sitkari can be practiced by anyone.

Shitali means "to cool" and Sitkari means "the action of cooling." Some modern yoga teachers believe these pranayamas will cool the body on a warm day. This works to some extent, but the original intention was something quite different.

Both pranayamas cool the tip of the tongue. The cool tip of the tongue is then touched lightly to the soft palate on the roof of the mouth. The soft palate is sensitive, so the touch of the cool tongue attracts the mind.

In normal consciousness, this attraction is mild, but with heightened sun energy and an expanded mind, the pull can be all-absorbing. **Just as the Ujjayi sound pulls the mind into an absorbed state, the cooling sensations on the soft palate pull the focus to the center of the head.** Everything else, even the body, can disappear from awareness.

To summarize, then, the main benefit of Shitali and Sitkari is this profound absorption, or deeply meditative state. The awareness is pulled up into the head and out of the realm of duality, which typically divides us and creates a state of conflict.

Practicing Shitali and Sitkari Pranayamas

1) Sit comfortably in a cross-legged position, kneeling, or on a chair, as described in Chapter 5. Wobble a little side to side and back to front to make sure your seat provides adequate and balanced support. If your seat does not support you properly, your abdominal muscles will have to work harder and will be less available for breathing.

2) Practice Dirgha and Ujjayi pranayamas for several minutes to warm up your body and mind.

3) Practice one or more rounds of Kapalabhati or Bhastrika until your mind feels expanded and open. If it feels appropriate, use a breath retention sequence with your energy-activating pranayamas. Sit quietly for a few moments to feel the effects before beginning Shitali or Sitkari. Relax into what you feel as best you can.

4) Exhale fully and extend your tongue straight out (not down) as far as you can. If you can, roll your tongue into a tube and practice Shitali by slowly inhaling through the tube.

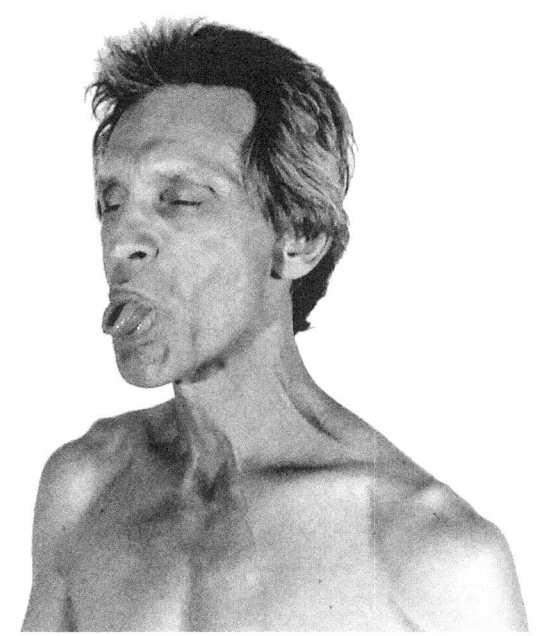
Rolling the tongue for Shitali Pranayama

If you cannot roll your tongue into a tube, practice Sitkari by lifting the tip of your tongue to make the shape of a bowl. Lower your upper lip until it is almost against the bowl, with a sliver of space between the top lip and the tongue. Inhale slowly.

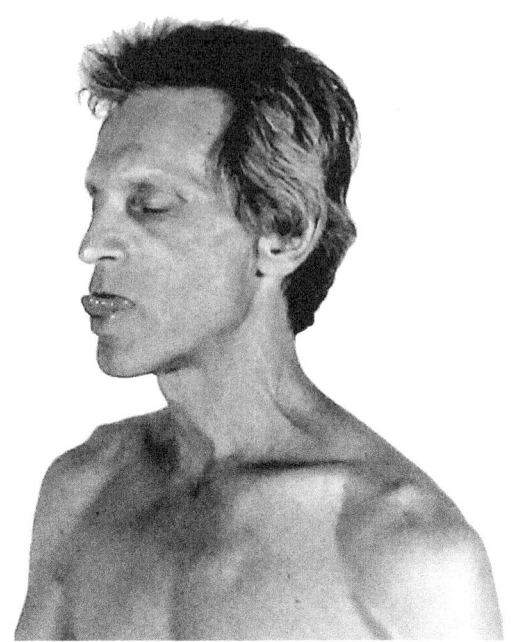

Making a bowl with the tongue for Sitkari Pranayama

Your goal with either technique is to cool the tip of your tongue as much as you can with your inhalation. Pull the breath in slowly and curl the tip of your tongue into the airstream.

5) When you have completely inhaled, pull your tongue into your mouth. Hold your breath as you lightly touch the tip of your tongue to the roof of your mouth. It's important to touch ever so lightly. Otherwise, the tongue warms up too quickly, and you lose the stimulation of the cool tongue.

The ideal place to touch the roof of the mouth is as far back as feels comfortable. The farther back in the mouth you touch, the more sensitive it is and the more likely it will draw your attention. Give all of your attention to what you feel at that point of contact between your tongue and the roof of your mouth.

6) When you become aware that you need to breathe, release the holding of the breath and tongue.

7) Taking a few normal breaths, see if your mind can stay focused on your soft palate where you feel the touch of your cool tongue.

8) After a few breaths, exhale, extend your tongue and repeat Shitali or Sitkari. If you prefer, you can take a full Dirgha breath before your next round of Shitali or Sitkari. Do at least three to five rounds of Shitali or Sitkari. You can do more if you'd like, but you'll want to try three to five rounds at least to feel the introversion and have it last for some time after the practice.

Note that there is no holding the breath out with Shitali and Sitkari, just holding in. The holding in happens in the background, while all of the attention remains on the point where the tongue connects with the roof of the mouth. You might sometimes hold longer than normal because you forget that you are holding. Suddenly your body tells you that you need to breathe, and you exhale.

There is a variation on Sitkari that you might wish to explore. It creates the same effect, just with a different technique. Instead of making a bowl with your tongue, place the tip of your tongue where your top and bottom teeth touch. You might have to open your jaw just a little bit. Press your tongue lightly here, open your lips, and slowly inhale, making a "sit" sound. Your intention is to cool the tip of your tongue. Then continue with step six above. This version may not feel good to students with sensitive teeth.

Practice Shitali and Sitkari for as long as you wish. To begin, we recommend at least three breaths, preferably five. If they are having the desired effect, there will be more and more time between rounds as your mind becomes absorbed for longer periods. As with Ujjayi, Shitali and Sitkari fade away and meditation (laya) remains.

Bhramari Pranayama: Bumble Bee Breath

The final pranayama for channeling energy, Bhramari, was given its name because of the high-pitched sound the yogi makes on the exhalation. Bhramari translates as "female bumblebee breath." In India, the bumblebees are more like Western yellow jackets, and the females are said to emit a higher pitch than the males. So the Sanskrit masters who named this breath were telling us to make the highest pitch possible.

The purpose of Bhramari is to capture your awareness and pull it deeply inside, creating an experience of laya, or meditation. If your Prana is heightened before doing Bhramari (through practicing Kapalabhati and Bhastrika), the Prana becomes the sound and the meditative effects will be even more profound.

Practicing Bhramari Pranayama

1) Sit comfortably in a cross-legged position, kneeling, or on a chair, as described in Chapter 5. Wobble a little side to side and back to front to make sure your seat provides adequate and balanced support. If your seat does not support you

properly, your abdominal muscles will have to work harder and will be less available for breathing.

2) Practice Dirgha and Ujjayi pranayamas for several minutes to warm up your body and mind.

3) Practice Kapalabhati or Bhastrika until your mind feels expanded and open. If it feels appropriate, use a breath retention sequence with your energy-activating pranayamas.

4) Sit quietly and feel the effects. Relax into what you feel as best you can.

5) Slowly raise the tip of your tongue to the roof of your mouth as far back as you can reach while still pressing up. Anchor your tongue here by pressing firmly.

6) Slowly inhale to capacity and then exhale making a loud, high-pitched sound through your throat and nose. Keep the sound as steady and high as you can through the whole exhale.

7) When all the breath is gone, hold out. You can keep your tongue in place or let it relax in your mouth. Let your attention follow the echo of the sound inside your head.

8) When your body reminds you that you need to breathe, release the holding and let your breath flow freely.

9) After a few breaths, lift your tongue, inhale fully, and repeat.

The first few times you practice Bhramari, your throat might tickle. This usually goes away quickly with regular practice. You might find that it returns if you go more than a few days without practicing. Too much Bhramari, especially if there is a tickle in your throat, can leave your throat irritated. Avoid this if you can, but if it does happen, drinking warm tea will help it pass quickly.

Yoganand

For a while, I practiced Bhramari because it was one of the principal pranayamas in the texts. It was not profound for me, until one day when I demonstrated for a class.

I sat down, took a deep breath in, pressed the tip of my tongue against the roof of my mouth, and began to make the sound on the exhalation. Suddenly the tone jumped an octave higher and I was gone from my body. I have no idea what happened, but when I opened my eyes, all I saw was a pack of strangers staring at me. It took three or four minutes for me to collect myself. That moment provided me a glimpse into the magic of Bhramari.

As you explore Bhramari for yourself, you will find that many factors affect the sound: how tightly you hold your jaw, and where and how firmly you press your tongue against the roof of your mouth. The physical vibration of the sound reverberates way up into the sinuses, stimulating sensors deep inside your head. You might find that with your tongue back farther, the sound seems higher. If you press fairly strongly, it might help to stabilize the sound at a higher pitch. Play around with different pitches, and something might suddenly open up and the sound might go higher. Stay there. Then look for a place to go even higher. It is an exploration into all the tensions and pressures, as well as the spaces, in the nasal cavity and the head. It is as though the inside of your head contains little corridors and rooms, and you can explore them through the sound.

To play with this a bit, place the tip of your tongue on the roof of your mouth and exhale, making a low sound that vibrates down in your jaw and between your teeth. Now do it again, this time making the sound vibrate slightly higher in your nose. Finally, take it as high as you can into your head and nasal passages.

You move the sound by tightening or relaxing subtle muscles. There is a little bit of skill involved, but eventually the sound becomes a point of intensity like a laser beam that you can aim wherever you want. You can move it around to find the highest pitch. Bring the sound to a high place and then explore relaxing around it to ensure that you are not carrying any unnecessary tension.

When students first try this breath, it tends to sound wimpy. Make it strong and loud. You might feel like you are just humming when you first begin. That's okay. Notice if you feel the vibration in your head and nasal passages. If not, raise the pitch. Make the highest pitch you can.

The directions say to exhale making the sound, then hold the breath out. Another option is to exhale making the sound, then immediately inhale and make another sound, skipping the breath retention. You could link three, four or five Bhramari breaths together, then hold the breath out. You could also make the sound on the inhalation. It's harder and feels a little strange, since the vibration tends to be more in your throat, but it's something you can play with.

Again, the point of Bhramari is to pull your attention into the top of your head and into a wordless place, where your thinking self can dissolve into a transcendent space.

Growing into the Energy-Channeling Pranayamas

When you are comfortable with the energy-channeling pranayamas, you can explore several variations of them:

1) Combine with energy-activating pranayamas. The techniques used to channel energy can be combined with those used to activate energy. For example, you can practice Kapalabhati and then exhale and hold out. When you need to breathe, take an Ujjayi inhale. Hold in, with the tip of your tongue pressed firmly against the roof of your mouth. When you need to breathe again, exhale with the Bhramari sound.

Any time you exhale after a sun-activating pranayama, you can do so with Ujjayi or Bhramari pranayama. When you inhale you can use Ujjayi, Shitali, or Sitkari.

2) Combine energy-channeling pranayamas together. The energy-channeling techniques can be combined to create a variation on these techniques. For example, you can inhale with Ujjayi, hold briefly and exhale with Bhramari. You could also inhale with Shitali or Sitkari and, after brief holding, exhale with the Bhramari sound.

3) Affirmations, prayers, visualizations. You can add affirmations, prayers, or visualizations to the energy-channeling pranayamas to deepen their effects. Here are some examples:

Affirmation: "I leave my small self behind and expand into my greater self."
Prayer: "I open myself to you, infinite spirit."
Visualization: Envision yourself as a morning fog dissolving into the space that contains it.

4) Meditation, posture flow, and relaxation. After energy-channeling pranayamas, you can sit for meditation or move into a posture flow that is inward-focused, keeping the priority on maintaining the internal awareness and absorption in sensation and flow. Profound experiences often occur when you lie in relaxation after dissolving the sun and moon.

5) Bandha mudras. Banda mudras are contractions inside the body that absorb the mind, and can be used to enhance the energy-channeling pranayamas. We will explain how to use them when we cover them in depth in Chapter 7.

6) Yoni mudra. Another way to work with the energy-channeling pranayamas is by adding a hand position called *Yoni* mudra. "Yoni" means "womb," and you essentially create a womblike space within your head by covering your eyes and ears with your fingers. There are lots of variations; we are going to learn a simple one here.

To add Yoni mudra to a pranayama, prepare for the practice by finding your stable seated position. Before beginning the pranayama, use your thumbs to firmly press the flaps in front of your ear openings over the holes to your inner ears. This should block out external sound. (Note that this is different from sticking your thumbs into your ears.) Rest your index and middle fingers lightly on your closed eyelids. Rest your two lower fingers on the lips, with the ring finger above the lips and the pinky finger below them.

Enhancing pranayama with Yoni Mudra

The most important elements of Yoni Mudra are closed ears and eyes and a comfortable hand position. The fingertips rest lightly, and they do not even have to be on the eyeballs. They can be on the top and bottom of the eyelids, so there's no pressure. The lower two fingers are much less important than the thumbs closing the ears and the fingers over the eyes. When you close your ears, you will find that you cannot hear. That is part of the effect. Also, the head tends to tilt back a bit, which is fine, but you do not want it to tilt too far back. That cramps the energy. Keep the back of your neck long.

As an example, this is how you would use Yoni Mudra with Bhramari pranayama: Take a slow, deep inhalation. Apply the hand position. Place the tip of your tongue on the roof of your mouth and then exhale through your nose, making the highest-pitched mosquito sound that you can. When you have finished exhaling, you can either hold out with the mudra or you can lower your hands to your lap.

Adding yoni mudra to the energy-channeling pranayamas drastically increases the introvertive effects of the pranayama, supporting the absorption and meditative state we are seeking with pranayama practice.

Whatever pranayamas you practice, do them responsibly. A little high energy adds enthusiasm and zest to your life. Too much makes you spacey and sets you up for disappointment. A little churning is a very spiritual opportunity. Too much leads to alienation and insecurity. Follow the guidelines given below and if the effects, physical or emotional, don't feel right, back off and seek help from a qualified teacher, therapist, or doctor.

General Guidelines for Pranayama

Yoganand

These guidelines came from Swami Kripalu, and I have found them very useful throughout the years. We intentionally saved them for the latter portion of the book with the hope that they will make more sense by the time you have reached this point. We wanted you to first gain an understanding of pranayama and ideally some practice with it to get the most from these tips.

1. Whenever possible, practice on an empty stomach.

An empty stomach allows you to breathe freely, and it also affects your flow of energy. One way to experience this is by doing five rounds of Anuloma Viloma. On the fifth round, time the length of your holding. Then eat three bites of food and try the pranayama again. You will probably find that your holding time has reduced by about 50%. Three bites is not enough to fill your stomach noticeably, so the shorter holding is not because you're too full to breathe freely. It is because your energy is tied up in digestion. So the more empty you are, the better your experience is, because of free breathing and the energy available to you.

Now, quite often, it is not realistic to practice on a completely empty stomach due to busy schedules. In that case, work from where you are. If you need to eat before practicing pranayama, eat lightly. You can still benefit from the practice, even though it will not be as powerful as if your stomach were empty. Having the stomach empty is optimal, but not always possible.

2. Never strain. Hold your breath only as long as is comfortable.

Some traditions say the longer you can hold, the better. They believe you are strengthening your will by doing so. That is true, but here we want pranayama to become an exercise in attunement. If you are straining and holding your breath too long, you are violating your body rather than connecting with it. That is just like going into a posture, saying, "His back is more arched than mine," and forcing your body beyond its limit of safety. When we do this in any aspect of yoga, we separate ourselves from the body and the body becomes abused in the process. Remember, pranayama practiced correctly facilitates attunement.

3. Increase practice time only when your practice is stable and regular.

Doing too much pranayama or increasing your practice too quickly can intensify or distort your emotions. Increased feelings of restlessness, anxiety, or irritability could be signs that you are overdoing it.

Irregular pranayama shocks the system. The more regularly you practice, the better. It is much more useful to do shorter, consistent practices than long, erratic practices. Regular daily practice is best. Recall Yoganand's story from Chapter 2:

Yoganand

I shared my experience of increasing my pranayama practice by one hour. I was supported in an ashram setting, so I could afford to have distorted, intensified emotions. I had gradually built up to six hours of pranayama practice at that time, but if I did six hours right now, it would be two or three days before I could talk. If you find that you are overdoing it, back off. It does not mean that you have to stop altogether. Just back off. Then, once your system acclimates to that level of practice, you can gradually increase again.

4. If you become tired, dizzy or nauseous, lie down and take slow, deep breaths.

Pranayama works by pulling your energy into a particular pattern. If you come to the practice with your energy disturbed, because you're worried about something or you haven't fully digested your last meal, this disturbance can generate nausea or dizziness. If you stop and take a couple of deep breaths, the nausea or dizziness will fade within a few seconds. If it doesn't, lie down for five or 10 breaths. Almost always, the system immediately rebalances.

6. Practice pranayama before or after postures, but before meditation.

For beginning practitioners, we recommend pranayama before postures. The postures help to ground the practitioner, so that he is better integrated at the end of his yoga. Those who are more advanced could choose to do either pranayama or postures first.

Yogananda

I found in my own practice that, if I did my pranayama first, my postures were deeper because the pranayama had opened me and created introversion. If I did my postures first, my pranayama was deeper because my postures had opened my body and awakened some energy. Whatever was second was better. So I did pranayama, postures, pranayama. I made a sandwich because I wanted it all.

Whether you do pranayama or postures first, save your meditation for last. Once your energy is flowing and you are attuned, meditation is easier. In fact, the higher your energy gets, assuming it is stable, the easier meditation is. If your energy is low, meditation is work. If you can keep your energy stable and raise it high, meditation happens automatically. You get sucked into it, and it is hard to come out. So work on building your container and raising the energy.

The problem for many of us is that we do not have the time to get our energy high and meditate, so we try to meditate with low energy. We get something from it, but meditation is most powerful when you can do the preparatory work that optimizes each stage.

7. Allow time for rest or introspection after your pranayama practice.

Yoganand

One of my favorite things to do after pranayama is walk in the woods early in the morning. After pranayama, I am sensitive and open. It is a time to study spiritual texts or read poetry. When I do pranayama and read the yogic texts, I gain insights that I do not see at any other time. Do you know why? Many of the texts were written by people who were in altered states. It's like trying to understand the writings of Timothy Leary. If the Bhagavad Gita *was written from an altered state, and you are in that state, there is a connection and a deeper understanding.*

We can get into trouble if we do 45 minutes of pranayama, rush out of the meditation room, grab a piece of toast, get in the car, and drive down the turnpike to work. That is when people say, "My pranayama causes so many problems!" It is not your pranayama causing trouble. It is the context. It's what's happening around your pranayama and the way you are putting it all together.

When you do your pranayama and you get into that sensitive, open space, take time to integrate that space into your consciousness. If you have to go to work, do not turn on rock music in the car. Do not turn on the news. Play some calming music and ease in. Drive the long way to work. Create some space between your pranayama and your need to function.

8. If you find pranayama uncomfortable during your menstrual period, do not do it.

There are many traditions that say you should never practice pranayama during menstruation. Some of them also say you should never practice asanas during menstruation. All of these traditions are taught by men, or by women who were taught by men. We have guided numerous female students in pranayama, and some of them find that the practice is no problem at all during menstruation. Some have said that Kapalabhati eases cramps and feels grounding. Other students avoid pranayama completely during menstruation. Explore it, and go with what works for you.

These eight pointers are meant to help you fine-tune your pranayama practice as you go. The closer you pay attention to your own experience, the easier it will be to adjust your practice to make it work best for you. Above all, pranayama is a practice of self-attunement and keen discernment.

The following guided pranayama experiences are available to support you:
- Yoganand's pranayama and yoga CDs, available at Pranakriya.com
- Allison's free pranayama downloads and yoga CD, available at AllisonGemmelLaframboise.com

CHAPTER SEVEN
MUDRAS

In ancient hatha yoga, three primary techniques were used to take yogis to the deepest places within themselves: *pratyahars, dharanas* and mudras. They all happened within asana practice and were enhanced by pranayama. We will briefly describe pratyahars and dharanas, and will spend the most time diving more deeply into mudras.

Pratyahar

"Pratyahar" literally means "to withdraw" or "to restrain." **The practice of pratyahar is to withdraw your attention from the senses, so it flows inward rather than outward.**

Take the sense of sight as an example. Normally, when we see something, we focus outward on what we see, or our reaction to it. Imagine you're walking through the mall, feeling completely content. Suddenly you see a sweater in a store window and become attracted to it. As you stare at the sweater, you can almost feel your energy flowing out of your eyes and into the sweater. As the sweater receives more of your energy, your ahankara loses energy. Eventually, the sweater might seem more real than you are. It might feel like a part of you is cut off and must be rejoined. You might even feel like, without that sweater, you will die.

Another reaction might be to resist it. You could look at the price tag and decide you can't afford it. You might struggle with yourself or you might struggle to get the sweater, but in either case the sweater has become extremely important.

What we have just described is a strong attraction. How many times a day does it happen in a lesser form? Walk down the snack aisle of a grocery store when you're hungry or drive through a neighborhood with gorgeous houses, and notice how many energy pulls you feel.

Pratyahar is making conscious the path from the seer, to the process of seeing, to the object being seen—and reversing it, so the awareness flows inward instead of outward. We can then become as enthusiastic about our inner self as we might be about an external object that we desire or fear.

> **Pratyahar**
>
> The practice of withdrawing one's attention from the senses, so it flows inward rather than outward.

Pratyahar can be practiced through any of the five senses, and the hatha yoga tradition offers many ways to explore it. For example, you might meditate for half an hour by withdrawing your awareness from the sense of hearing, listening first to loud external sounds, then gradually to more subtle external sounds, and, eventually, to inner sounds. Finally you shift your attention to the one who hears—the self.

In another example, you might move from one technique to another. You begin by listening first to external sounds, then take your attention to the eyes. Feel the brow, lids, lashes, surface of the eyes, iris muscles, and interior of the eyes. Shift to the process of seeing, and notice the colors or areas of brightness and darkness in your inner field of vision. Then take the attention to the one who sees.

There are many ways to practice pratyahar, and the common thread is withdrawing the senses so attention flows inward.

Dharana

Whereas pratyahar is focusing one's awareness on the senses, **dharana is the practice of concentrating on abstract objects, ideas, or movements inside the body.** Examples of dharana include focusing on an area inside the body, such as the lower abdomen or the inside of the skull; noticing sensations inside the body, such as the emptiness in the belly when one is hungry or the sensation of stretch in a muscle; feeling the movement in the chest when you breathe or the beating of your heart; visualizing the Om symbol inside a triangle in the third-eye center; feeling the presence of a deity; or making a journey through an inner landscape to visit a sacred place.

> **Dharana**
> The practice of focusing one's attention on an abstract object, idea, or movement inside the body.

As with pratyahars, there are countless possible dharanas. The commonality here is focusing on an abstract object, idea, or inner movement.

Mudra

The Sanskrit word "mudra" has a long list of definitions and appears in many Indian spiritual traditions. In tantric hatha yoga, **a mudra is a contraction inside the body that absorbs all the attention.** The mudra energizes the part of the body where the contraction is happening and makes it feel extremely alive. This aliveness might reveal hidden tensions or fears held in that part of the body.

Through the practice of mudra, tensions can be released and fears rise into awareness so they can be witnessed. When a yoga technique makes us feel more alive, we see the fears that previously caused us to shut down. Sometimes we not only recognize the fears, but also the ways in which we have shut down to them. With this new self-knowledge, we have a decision to remain closed or choose to open.

> **Mudra**
>
> A contraction inside the body that absorbs the attention of the mind.

Manduki mudra is a simple technique that illustrates how all mudras work. "Manduki" means "frog" in Sanskrit, a reference to the tongue becoming long and thin, like that of a tree frog, as it stretches upward to touch the roof of the mouth. Read through the instructions, then try it.

Manduki Mudra

1) Sit in a comfortable, stable position with your eyes closed. Take a few deep breaths and notice how your body feels and how your attention spreads through your body.

2) Take the tip of your tongue to the roof of your mouth and touch it there as lightly as you can. Notice what happens to your attention as soon as your tongue makes contact. Most likely, all of your attention will go to the contact point between your tongue and the roof of your mouth. If you slowly move your tongue towards the back of your mouth, you will start to feel a stretch on the bottom of your tongue, or you might feel yourself gagging or choking. These sensations might bring heightened emotions. Explore these nuances for about one minute.

3) Release your tongue and take several breaths. Notice whether your attention externalizes quickly or slowly. Can you detect stages in the process of coming back to the external world?

Practitioners who have experienced a trauma related to the mouth or throat might be reminded of it when doing Manduki mudra, and possibly even relive it through the practice. This would more likely occur if the practitioner had opened the body with asanas and raised the energy with pranayama before doing the mudra. **When we are able to witness the emotions arise, while affirming that we are in a safe space and in control, that's when a layer of past trauma can be healed and integrated.**

Pratyahars, dharanas, and mudras can be practiced willfully and consciously, as we have illustrated here. Typically, this was the first level of deeper practice in ancient yoga schools. In later stages of practice, yogis experienced pratyahar, dharana, and mudra spontaneously.

Students preparing for spontaneous practice would live celibate lifestyles, practice asana and pranayama daily, and eat quite moderately. Swami Kripalu taught that a yogi practicing this way never completely sated his hunger. He left each meal feeling a bit hungry, and this hunger remained in the background as he went through his day, making it easy for insecurities and fears to be triggered. The celibacy, asana, and pranayama contributed to this state of heightened energy and sensitivity, grounding the yogi's attention in the body and the present moment, regardless of what he was doing.

When the practitioner grew steady in this state, he was ready for spontaneous practice. After asana and pranayama, he might have felt, for example, an emptiness in his belly that he associated with hunger. Practicing dharana in this case would mean feeling the sensation of emptiness and observing whatever the mind associated with that emptiness—perhaps times in the past when his food needs were not met, or experiences in which he felt weak or helpless. As he continued the practice, the experience would evolve. The hunger might fade and the emptiness in the belly might become a vast sense of openness and vulnerability. In a meditative state, openness and vulnerability can easily become a connection with spirit. In openness, the ahankara partially dissolves. In vulnerability, we can be drawn to take refuge in spirit.

Spontaneous pratyahar might occur while holding breath retention, as the student finds the inner gaze pulled to the spot between the eyebrows and feels that the whole self is flowing like water into this spot.

The most blatant example of a spontaneous mudra is sexual arousal. One moment, your genitals feel no different from the rest of your body. The next moment, a rush of energy flows into them. Unless you consciously push the sensations away, your attention gets pulled right to the arousal, and the experience can be totally absorbing.

Sexual energy is quite often used in the hatha yoga texts around descriptions of the mudras, but this does not mean that the mudras are sexual. The similarity lies in taking energy to that part of your body by contracting it. That contraction stimulates new energy, at the same time that it receives existing energy that is already circulating in your system. The place of contraction becomes a focal point for all your attention.

The *Hatha Yoga Pradipika* describes 10 mudras. Some of the other texts describe as many as 25. All but three of these mudras must happen spontaneously, and cannot be engaged willfully; rather, the body must be conditioned for them. The body must be extremely open with an abundance of energy moving inside. Like an advanced asana, these mudras are useless until you have prepared your body for them.

The three mudras labeled with an * in Figure 14 are foundational mudras that can be engaged willfully and are usually taught to the advanced student of pranayama. They are *Mula Bandha, Uddiyana Bandha,* and *Jalandhara Bandha*.

The word "bandha" means "to bind" or "to lock." These mudras lock the breath. This means that, when you are holding them appropriately, it is impossible to breathe. As we will learn, this is a major distinction between the traditional locks and the locks taught in yoga classes today.

We will spend the most time on Mula Bandha, the root lock, and then move onto Uddiyana Bandha, the stomach lock, and Jalandhara Bandha, the throat lock. Once you become proficient with the root lock, it's fairly easy to work with the others. As you feel comfortable with the locks, you can incorporate them into pranayama practice.

> Figure 14. Ten mudras in the *Hatha Yoga Pradipika:*
>
> Shakti Chalana Mudra
> Mula Bandha Mudra (Root lock) *
> Vajroli Mudra
> Maha Mudra
> Maha Vedha Mudra
> Maha Bandha Mudra
> Uddiyana Bandha Mudra (Stomach lock) *
> Viparita Karni Mudra
> Jalandhara Bandha Mudra (Throat lock) *
> Kechari Mudra

Swami Kripalu taught that there is only one mudra—it just happens in 10 different places. The same is true of the locks: There is only one lock; it just happens in three different places.

Mula Bandha Mudra: The Root Lock

Many modern yoga traditions teach Mula Bandha as an engagement of the pelvic floor used to stabilize the body in standing postures. Also referred to as stabilizing or strengthening the core, this is a wonderful technique, but we encourage you to set it aside for now. We are referring to Mula Bandha as something radically different here.

Yoganand

The ancient hatha yoga texts refer to Mula Bandha as a technique that can only be explored in seated and forward-bending postures. They do not work in back bending, twisting, or standing postures.

Sometimes people take an esoteric secret of yoga and apply it in a way that it was never intended. Then they treat that application as though it is the end point when, in fact, the teaching was meant to be a doorway to a very deep place.

Swami Kripalu gave a beautiful example of this with the Bhagavad Gita. *He said the* Bhagavad Gita *is one of the deepest scriptures of surrender yoga. It is like a sword so powerful that you could take it into the battlefield and chop off heads. You could take that same sword, however, use it to chop vegetables, and never know the full spectrum of its potential.*

Applying this lesson to Mula Bandha Mudra, we understand that **engaging the pelvic muscles in asanas is a fine application of this practice, but there is a whole other realm to explore as well.** It can be helpful to think of Mula Bandha as two practices, one for householders and the other for renunciates. **The householder version of Mula Bandha creates strength and stability** through the support of the abdominal and pelvic muscles in strenuous postures. This might translate off the mat as a feeling of strength radiating from the belly, creating a sense of confidence.

The traditional form of Mula Bandha, practiced by renunciates, opens the belly, releasing a flow of primal energy from the pelvis. This energy can reveal strong emotions and trigger past traumas and insecurities. By witnessing the effects of the mudra in pranayama practice, the sense of self is transformed. When this happens, the practice can produce a feeling of expansion and freedom.

The householder practice of Mula Bandha validates ahankara; the renunciate version dissolves ahankara. For most people today, validating ahankara is more useful. However, to understand deeper pranayama practice, it's helpful to understand the older technique of Mula Bandha mudra, and perhaps even experiment with it in your practice.

Mula Bhanda Technique

1) Find a seated position that works well for your body. We recommend Padmasana (Lotus pose) or Swastikasana, if you can sit comfortably without rounding your back. These postures allow you to press your knees toward each other and get a strong foundation from which the lock can spring upward. If, however, you have to round your back in order to sit in these asanas, choose any seated position from Chapter 5 that works better for your body.

Padmasana (Lotus pose)

Swastikasana

2) Sit for a moment with a straight back, without elongating. Notice how it feels. Now lengthen through your waist and your torso, and notice the difference. When you elongate, that elongation generates sensation. That becomes a channel through which energy can move.

3) Once you've found your seated position, exhale completely and hold your breath out. Lengthen fully through your torso until you feel a vacuum in your abdomen. Then lift, rather than squeeze, your pelvic floor as high as you can, as if it could fill that vacuum. You will feel your buttocks tighten and your belly pull in; let that be an effect of the lifting. Try to lift your pelvic floor all the way up to your solar plexus, but don't let your ribs drop down. Instead, add the lock to the upward lengthening of your torso.

4) Hold the breath out as long as you can. When you need to breathe, release the pelvic floor and let the breath flow in. While you are holding, you might notice that all of your attention goes to the work you are doing and the feeling of the lock. After you release the lock, you might notice that your pelvis and abdomen feel more alive.

The instructions here describe Mula Bandha mudra with external breath retention. It can be practiced with internal breath retention as well, but it is less effective in the beginning.

Initially, holding the root lock requires work, and you don't usually feel much. It can also feel weird or vague. This is all normal. As you practice, the muscles used to engage the lock become stronger and more efficient. The point of concentration and contraction becomes more refined. You also develop the neural connections required to engage the parts of your body that you want to engage, and relax the parts that you want to relax.

When first starting out, work with a strong contraction, and lift everything up. Anatomically, this means lifting the following muscles:

1) **Pelvic floor muscles:** These are the muscles you contract when trying not to urinate or when practicing Kegal exercises. When you engage them for Mula Bhanda, focus more on lifting, less on squeezing.

2**) Transverse abdominis**: The deepest layer of abdominal muscle, the transverse abdominis wraps around the belly horizontally, like a girdle. When you try to lift the pelvic floor as high as possible, this sheet of muscle will engage all the way around.

3) **Psoas muscle:** The psoas muscle is a rope-like muscle that runs from the spine to the top of the femur (thigh bone). The psoas muscles will engage when you lift the pelvic floor and lengthen your waist.

4) **Gluteus maximus:** The largest muscle in the buttocks, this muscle will contract to stabilize the pelvis.

On a physical level, a strong upward lift strengthens and opens the pelvis, and that effect alone can be very valuable. Beyond the physical benefit, beginning with a strong contraction provides a wide range of more subtle engagement to explore later. Once it feels easy to work with the lock, then you can choose to make it soft if you find that a softer contraction best absorbs your mind. If you never experiment with the strongest contraction, however, you limit your range of exploration. You might end up with a soft contraction, because it's all you know, not because you chose it. This is why we encourage a strong contraction with a forceful upward pull when you are learning the locks.

Mula Bandha is not something you do and then you're done. It is a rich inquiry to explore. Recall our discussion of the Ujjayi breath in Chapter 6. We know how to create the sound by reaching for its intention: to conquer the mind. This allows us to explore variations of Ujjayi breathing. Mula Bandha can also be explored by way of its intention: to create a point of strong contraction inside the pelvis that can capture your mind. Do it as intensely as it needs to be done to generate the engagement and focus of attention.

As you eventually refine the technique, the lock becomes a line of strong sensation behind and below the navel. It becomes a point on which you can focus and a doorway to your unfolding.

Enlivening the Pelvis

The physiological level of the locks is just the foundation. Many more layers await exploration. The hatha yoga model with which we are working teaches that our anger, fear, and sexual energy spring from the pelvis. Typically, these forces threaten us, so we tighten the abdomen and pelvis to suppress them. The mind pushes so many energies down into the darkness; the ahankara pushes so many energies down into the realm of apana. What we are trying to do with Mula Bandha mudra is reach down with prana, grab apana, and say, "Let me see you!" That's why the root lock is all about a strong, upward pull, not pulling up a little bit and rounding down a little bit to meet in the middle. Practiced fully, the root lock not only happens down in the pelvis, it also reaches way up into the belly, because there is an abdominal engagement to keep everything lifted. **As you do this work to open the pelvis and the belly, be aware of what's happening on the levels beyond the physical. The light of awareness and the energies that are stored in the pelvis and abdomen are revealed to us, too.**

For the root lock to be fully applied, there must be no armor in the pelvis. At the same time, the root lock is a powerful technique for releasing armor in the pelvis. **If there were no armor in the pelvis and the pelvis was fully alive, what would that feel like?** You might get in touch with aspects of your body that you don't usually feel. This is a part of the body we rarely ever move. When we do, we enliven it, and it feels connected with the rest of us.

In the lifting, there is an energizing. Gravity is continually pulling our insides down. If we turn that around and start to pull them up, it generates sensation and vitality. The pelvis starts to come alive. Will you encounter shame in the pelvis? Will you experience weirdness? Might you feel sexual arousal? Yes, you might experience all sorts of things. Just watch. Notice the reaction, the resistance, and the way you frame your experience. **Do not make it mean anything. Just let it be.** If you come to a point where you're fighting yourself, you've gone too far. It should be work but it should not be a struggle, and you don't want to expend energy trying to force it to happen with your mind. Say yes to the lock. Say yes to aliveness, vitality, and energy moving.

Mula Bandha is no more sexual than a pelvic exam performed in a doctor's office, but it has the power to trigger sexual feelings and associations. The challenge is to witness all that arises from the mudra in a way that allows sexual trauma to heal, and supports the development of a new, healthier relationship with the sexual self.

How can you be sure you are practicing the lock correctly? First, if the lock is applied properly, you won't be able to breathe.

Swami Kripalu said something about the root lock that I have verified in my own practice. If the root lock is fully applied, you cannot breathe. This happens because the lengthening and lifting engages so many of the breathing muscles that the ribs can't move. This might not happen in the beginning, but rather as the lock becomes more refined. It becomes more and more difficult to breathe, to the point where the lock generates breath retention. This is why I say the traditional hatha yoga application taught in the texts does not work in standing postures or back bending postures. Although the root lock can be done with the lungs full of air, it is strongest when the lungs are empty. I encourage beginning students to practice only with external retention until the lock is strong.

Shiva Lingham – Core Contraction

At first, the locks tend to feel very amorphous, but once the root lock is working and you are relaxing everything around it, it feels like a Shiva Lingham, the column of stone that symbolizes the Hindu God Shiva. In other words, **you will experience a core contraction from your pelvic floor up through the center of your body to your navel.**

If you are a male and you engage the lock properly, it will feel like you have an erection, except it will be inside your belly rather than outside. If you are a female, it will feel like you are having intercourse. Again, the locks are not sexual. They simply generate sensations and perhaps feelings that might bring up strong associations.

When you add the stomach lock, the Shiva Lingham continues from the navel up to the heart. When you add the throat lock, it grows further up the core to the throat.

When you look at the statue, you see that the Shiva Lingham goes right up through the core of the yogi's body. That symbolizes the three locks. Everything else relaxes around them, but this column of intensity rises right up through the center of the body. The more you can relax around it and the more precisely it is defined, the longer you can hold the locks, which leads to deeper concentration.

When you hold your breath out and engage the root lock, there is a tendency to round the shoulders down, meeting in the middle. To work toward the sensation of the Shiva Lingham, keep your torso long and pull up. Because most of us only use these muscles automatically in everyday activities, such as walking, we usually have no conscious awareness of them. When we tell them to contract, they don't know how. That's why it takes time to grow into the root lock and, eventually, the stomach and throat locks.

The Shiva Lingham symbolizes the core contraction through the center of the yogi's body that is created by the locks.

Uddiyana Bandha Mudra: The Stomach Lock

We have learned that the root lock builds a bridge from the pelvis up to the navel. The stomach lock continues that bridge from the navel up to the heart. **To engage the stomach lock, think of taking your navel and pulling it up under your ribs.** Some teachers say to pull it back toward your spine, but we find that up works better. If you pull your belly in, it doesn't necessarily go up, but if you pull up, it will also go in. **With all the locks, we want an upward pull through the core of the body, while the outer part of the body relaxes.**

The stomach lock is easiest to practice while holding the breath out. Holding the breath in, you can engage the stomach lock partially, but you cannot engage it completely because of the cushion of air in the lungs. The benefit of a partial stomach lock on internal retention is that it stimulates the heart and creates a pressure in the chest, which serves as its own mudra, or point of focus.

As with the root lock, many people tend to round their backs when practicing the stomach lock. Something must move downward to balance the movement upward, so the effect is neutralized. When you are doing the stomach lock, stay tall. Let everything down below come up.

The stomach lock is most powerful on an empty stomach, so it is best to practice it in the morning before eating. In fact, in the yoga world, there is a magical time to practice pranayama and mudras, and that is between bowel movement and breakfast. That is when you are most empty. When you are empty, energy can flow more easily. The locks or Nauli kriya done at that time are profound and amazing.

Practicing them after eating will not have as pronounced an effect, but it is not always practical to practice on an empty belly. When that is the case, eating very lightly is best.

Jalandhara Bandha Mudra: The Throat Lock

The throat lock is the most elusive of the three locks. There are three parts to this mudra. They can be applied in any order or all at once.

1) Half swallow, lift your Adam's apple, and hold it up.

2) Tuck your chin and reach up through the crown of your head to lengthen your neck.

3) Press the tip of your tongue against the roof of your mouth as far back as you can reach.

Let's look at each part:

1) **Half swallow:** When you swallow, your Adam's apple goes up, then comes back down. To feel this, hold your fingers gently against your Adam's apple and swallow. With a little practice, you will be able to interrupt the swallow and keep the Adam's apple lifted. Do not hold it up with your fingers; only use your fingers to feel the Adam's apple moving. As long as you hold your Adam's apple up, you cannot breathe. The throat lock can be used when holding the breath in or holding it out (more on this later).

2) **Tuck your chin:** This does not mean tilt your head forward. It means pull your chin straight back as if you were going to touch the bottom of your chin to your Adam's

apple. In old yoga books, you might see photos of yoga masters demonstrating Jalandhara Bandha Mudra with their upper backs rounded and their heads dropped forward. The head position aligns the tongue. The rounded position might be appropriate for masters, but most beginning students should practice with the head lifted. This will make more sense as we discuss the third element of the throat lock.

3) **Press the tip of your tongue against the roof of your mouth as far back as you can reach.** When we push the tip of the tongue against the roof of the mouth, the tongue becomes firm and, when we reach it back, we create stretch in the tongue. When we engage all three bandhas, we feel the line of upward pull extend all the way up into the tongue. Practicing the throat lock, we reach the tongue back as far as it will go while still pressing up. (If we reach too far back, it curls down.) Then we position the head so the tongue points straight up, extending the line from the two locks below.

There are three tongue and head positions. If the tongue reaches only to the hard palate, the head is fully upright when the chin is tucked. If the tongue reaches as far as the soft palate, the head will tilt a little forward when the tongue points up. In the third position, the tongue goes behind the soft palate and presses up into the pharynx. To point the tongue upward, the head moves much more forward.

After breath retention, release the three parts of the bandha mudra and let the breath flow in or out.

As with the other two locks, avoid rounding the neck and back. Rounding counteracts the upward pull that we are trying to create. **If you were to sit against a wall and engage the locks correctly, you would not move away from the wall. If you have built a strong charge of energy and focus**

all your attention on the upward pull inside, you become that upward pull. You become the column of light in the center of the body. That is the goal of the locks.

Yoganand

Some people think that the primary purpose of the throat lock is to help them hold the breath longer. I disagree. When it is used to hold the breath longer, the holding can turn into a struggle. Once the yogi starts to struggle with himself, then he is out of sushumna. He is back in the world and back in his mind. You should never hold your breath to a point where you are struggling with yourself. I believe the throat lock is intended to increase the yogi's ability to feel a channel connecting the pelvis with the crown of the head, not to increase holding time. Remember, there is no benefit to depriving your brain cells of oxygen.

Because the throat and stomach locks are difficult to grasp, it is helpful to work with the root lock first. When the root lock pops in easily and strongly, then, as Swami Kripalu said, there is only one lock, it just happens in three different places. The root lock is the easiest one to grasp and it can give a sense of what the others should feel like.

Breath Retention and the Locks

Yoganand

I have experimented with combining breath work and the locks in many different ways. The way that I love to practice, which best fits yoga philosophy as I understand it, is to exhale fully and hold the breath out. While holding out, I engage the locks. I like to first hold my breath out with my attention going down, then release the locks, inhale, and hold the breath in, allowing my attention to rise up.

When you hold the breath out, the complete emptiness in the lower torso creates a strong sensation that inevitably grabs the attention. Then, when we inhale, all that sensation disappears and we experience the awareness automatically rising up.

When practicing several rounds of pranayama, progressions can help to deepen the experience.

If I am going to lead my students in three rounds of Kapalabhati, I try to deepen them so that each one is a little bit more engaged than the one before. For the first two rounds, I don't have them engage the locks, but I direct them where to focus their attention during breath retention. After the first round of Kapalabhati, I usually have my students hold the breath out, focusing their attention in the pelvis, then inhale, hold in, and focus on the crown of the head. This technique often creates a feeling of expansion or a rising upward. For the second round of Kapalabhati, I do the same thing, except I have them focus on the third eye point between the eyebrows during the internal holding, rather than focusing on the crown.

For the third round of Kapalabhati, I direct them to engage the locks during the external breath retention. Once they are using the locks, I stop telling them where to focus, because the locks will dictate that. If you are doing just the root lock, your attention will go down to the pelvis, guaranteed. If you are doing the throat lock, your awareness will tend to go up. If you are doing the stomach lock, it will tend to be in the stomach.

We have been encouraging you to develop a solid foundation with the root lock before working with the others. Interestingly, however, if you are proficient with the root lock and you focus exclusively on engaging the stomach lock, the root lock will happen, too. In the same way, a strong throat lock will cause the other two locks to pop in, though they might not be as strong as they would be if they were the primary focus. The locks are linked together, and rise from the pelvis up through the core of the body.

Letting Go of Expectations

Visualizations can be used when working with the locks. You might imagine light rising from the pelvis to the crown of the head. If that deepens your experience, it's fine to work with it. Quite often, however, expecting something specific to happen distracts us from what is actually happening.

Let go of trying to see anything specific. Let go of trying to make energy flow in a particular way. If you sit with your eyes closed, straighten your back, and elongate through your waist, you can create a sensation of stretch. That sensation could be considered a channel of energy. You don't have to visualize light; the sensation can be interpreted as light.

We have touched upon some visualization exercises in this book but, in most traditional schools of hatha yoga, there is very little focus on visualization and much more focus on creation. Create sensation. Create energy. Create a feeling. The visualization grows out of that creation.

Yoganand

When I practice Bhastrika, it can feel like sparks are flying out of my fingertips. If anyone were in the room with me, they would not see sparks, but it feels as if there are sparks. I could try to willfully visualize sparks until I turn blue in the face, but the pranayama giving me the feeling of the sparks is much more real.

So, let go of trying to make something happen. **It's a far deeper experience to open the body and then dive in to see what's there—not what's supposed to be there, but what is actually there.**

The chakras provide a good example of this. They are sometimes pictured as lotuses, with little animals, ladies with swords, and Sanskrit letters on the petals. These are nice focal points for dharana experiences, in which you concentrate on visualizing these images to increase your discrimination and your ability to hold the mind steady. But these images might not be related at all to what's inside you.

How many chakras are there? There are texts that describe one, two, three, five, seven, nine, or 11. Many texts describe 14. There are hatha yoga texts that do not mention chakras at all. Different people explored their own inner worlds and discovered different things. The animals and the ladies with the swords are symbolic of energies. One yogi goes inside and sees it one way. Another yogi goes inside and sees it a different way.

If a group of people tasted the same chocolate cake and was asked to write 10 sentences describing what it tasted like, what are the chances of two people writing the exact same sentences? Similar words would appear, but the chances of two people writing exactly the same thing are very slim. So, when we do something even more vague than tasting chocolate cake, such as responding to the guidance, "Go inside and feel," what are the chances of your experience being exactly the same as someone else's?

We can use what has been written as models and possibilities, but keep in mind that they are just that. It might be completely different for you. If you go looking for something particular, it's unlikely that you will find it. There's no need to seek the city of jewels, for example, as the third chakra is described. Instead, go with what's real. *What do you really feel inside?*

Growing Into the Locks

As you open to what is truly happening in your body through time and consistent practice, you grow into the locks. **It is your own unique exploration, a journey that only you can take, and one that is full of possibilities.**

Consider the root lock. No one else can tell you exactly which muscles engage the root lock. Someone might tell you which muscles are in that area of the body, but you would have to use electrodes to know which ones specifically create the lock. Earlier, we discussed the muscles to pull up when you are beginning the root lock, but that's a starting point, and it's not the same for everyone. At some point, it becomes your own.

Let's say that 10 muscles are involved in the root lock and three or four of them are lethargic. They never exercise, so they're weak. They might engage the first couple of times you apply the lock in a practice session and, after they tire, those muscles drop out. Maybe two other muscles are holding some tension from being the same length for a long time. They have started to atrophy and have lost their ability to move. Are they going to stand in the way of your experiencing the locks? Probably. Perhaps a couple of other muscles do not know how to move in the way they need to move to create the lock, because they typically move only through an automatic process like peristalsis. They have never been moved willfully, so they do not know how. These muscles have only been told by the unconscious what to do, and suddenly the mind is saying, "You should engage." But they don't know how to engage.

Over the course of a few weeks or a few months of daily practice, your relationship with the locks changes drastically. A process governed by the autonomic nervous system can be made willful. As the lock becomes more proficient and you start feeling more alive in the pelvis and the abdomen, it can feel weird and possibly scary. What if your food starts digesting differently? What if your elimination gets stronger? The root lock can improve your elimination by toning the colon and making the colon work better. That might mean that you have more vitality and an extra little kick in your step. As the pelvis becomes more alive, it might feel as if it moves differently, which could affect your walking or your dancing. With more freedom in your body, you become more connected with your core, and you can dance or run with more energy.

What about the impact of regular practice on stressful situations, such as a meeting with your boss? Do you ever get discomfort in your belly and weakness in your knees in what feels like a dangerous situation? If the pelvis is more open, it's possible that those sensations could be amplified. It's also possible that you could feel stronger and more powerful. Either could happen. Both are likely to change you.

What about your sexual experience? Could the root lock change your sexual experience? It certainly could. For someone who is sexually repressed, for example, the root lock might bring up feelings that were uncomfortable to deal with. He may not have even known the feelings were there, but the lock could bring them to the surface, where he could see them, integrate them, and move forward with a healthier relationship to his sexuality.

Thus, this simple little contraction could possibly change your life. It's that powerful. But it doesn't just happen overnight. It's not a matter of "I learned the root lock and I am done." The root lock is an immense territory to explore and discover.

From Willful to Spontaneous

At first, the locks are work. As you become proficient with them, the pelvis, solar plexus, and throat open, and the locks can happen by themselves. When they do, they will not necessarily happen the same way they did when you practiced them willfully. You learn to consciously engage the lock one way, and then, when you sit down to practice one day and they happen automatically, you say, "Even if I tried, I couldn't do it exactly like this." **When this happens, you are beginning to move from the mudras that can be practiced willfully to the mudras that happen only spontaneously.**

When the locks start to take on a life of their own, they will begin to feel much different. If you find that you are fully open and giving yourself completely to the lock and it is showing up differently, that means something has let go, opened, or shifted. Explore that. It's not about descending down into the pelvis, beating everything into submission, and forcing something to happen. It's a process of unfolding, revealing a part of your body and your psyche that has been shut off. **When the locks engage automatically, the body has become fully alive.**

The Mudras and Witness Consciousness

When we take our awareness inside with practices like mudras, old memories and emotions tend to surface as well. If we can soften, then all the memories and everything linked to them can rise to the surface, and we are presented with an opportunity for integration and healing.

Think about anger. Whatever you feel angry about is linked to all the other angry feelings you've had in your life. The same is true of fear. Every fear you experience is linked to every other fear you have ever experienced. Imagine you're sitting in your boss's office and he's telling you something you don't want to hear, and suddenly you're in fifth grade in the principal's office at school. Then you are in your car by the interstate, and a policeman is handing you a speeding ticket. You connect with every place where you have felt fear. We armor against fear and, when something fearful happens, we respond to it in the same way that we respond to all the other fears. It might be scaled down because there is some distance between the two situations, but they're all related.

In the chapter about the shatkriyas, we talked about the Pashupatas, who viewed fear as God. Suppose a person finds himself in a situation in which he is afraid because someone yelled at him. He might first feel anger, then fear. If he can close his eyes, let go of the person yelling, and just be with the fear, the links to other fearful experiences would start to become visible. He would become that fifth grader in the principal's office. He would become that three-year-old child whose parents lost him at the grocery store. He would remember waking up in the middle of the night to an animal howling outside his window. Every fear he ever felt could potentially come into his mind, because he has taken the current fear and separated it from the source.

His mind will start looking for the source. It will bring up past fears for him to see, asking "Is this it?" As this happens, he is presented with an opportunity for spiritual growth if he can step into witness consciousness and simply observe. **If he can watch those fears objectively, without judging them or reacting to them, there is an enormous**

potential for integration, healing, and increased self-knowledge.

In the same way, when we go into the body, particularly in the pelvis or another part of the trunk, we can experience sensations and emotions connected to our past. When energy is generated through mudras and pranayamas, it's an opportunity to experience the sensations and just be with them, without censoring or judging, and allow the past to unfold. That is the power of the locks.

Yoganand

Sometimes, when I do the locks, I come out of my practice feeling like I'm about four years old. I regress. Regression can happen easily with the locks, because the insides are unfolding. That has potential for tremendous healing.

This is what we risk missing when we limit the locks to "I engage Mula Bandha in Warrior I for safe and strong alignment." There's nothing wrong with that, but it takes the locks in a completely different direction. These practices were originally meant to provide access to a much more powerful place. The locks are mysteries. They are secret doorways into our unfolding and healing.

Beyond the Foundational Mudras

Yoganand

When I teach students about the three locks, someone often asks, "Are we going to learn the other mudras?" The mudras are the most esoteric aspect of hatha yoga. Only three of them can be engaged willfully. Some of them are very vague to describe and, if I talk about them to people who have not experienced them, they don't make sense. Some of them are just bizarre. But we will tell you a little bit about the mudras here so you have a better understanding of their context and potential.

The word "kundalini" is used in many different contexts. Kundalini is essentially sun energy from apana that can flood the ahankara and dissolve it. Sexual energy can do that, which is why sexual energy is often associated with kundalini. Some people say sexual energy is kundalini. Some say kundalini is sexual energy that has been sublimated into a neutral, pure energy. There are many different ways to frame it.

In a normal state of awareness, our whole body feels fairly uniform. When kundalini energy or sexual energy flows into the genitals, they become fully alive. **The yogis discovered ways to make that same energy flow into other places in their bodies, and that is exactly what the mudras are.**

If a bodily region cannot hold that level of aliveness, the energy remains sexual in nature and eventually returns to the pelvis, seeking external expression. The farther the energy lifts from the pelvis, the less it is perceived as sexual energy, sometimes manifesting as anger or fear. When the body absorbs the energy as aliveness, in the way the ancients desired, it can be experienced as joy, love, or pure bliss.

Traditionally, the only person who did this type of sadhana was a monk. You can imagine how alarming it would be for a celibate monk, who had renounced sex for life, to experience intense sexual energy arising in different parts of his body. His teacher would say, "Just practice watching the energy. It feels like sexual energy, but it's not."

The shatkriyas work from the pelvis all the way up into the head. **The mudras also work from the pelvis up to the head, as do the pranayamas.** These techniques give us wave after wave of stimulation moving upward. By activating these waves of energy with the shatkriyas, the pranayamas, and eventually the mudras, the yogis would find the same experience happening over and over again: In different parts of the body along the trunk, they experienced a profound level of arousal.

When the arousal is focused at a certain place, it draws the yogi to move and stimulate that part of the body. It is so intense that he can't sit still. If that sexual energy goes into the abdominal rectus muscle, Nauli kriya happens spontaneously. It's like reaching the point during sex where your body starts vibrating by itself, except it happens in different places in the body. That place and that occurrence is the mudra.

A mudra at its most powerful is essentially a sexual experience, but it is not sexual. It is an organ so fully alive that it is pulsing and wanting to discharge energy. There is nothing inherently sexual about that. The only reason we refer to it as sexual is because the one place in which we normally experience anything like this is in sexual experiences.

Figure 15. The mudras open a channel from the pelvis to the crown of the head.

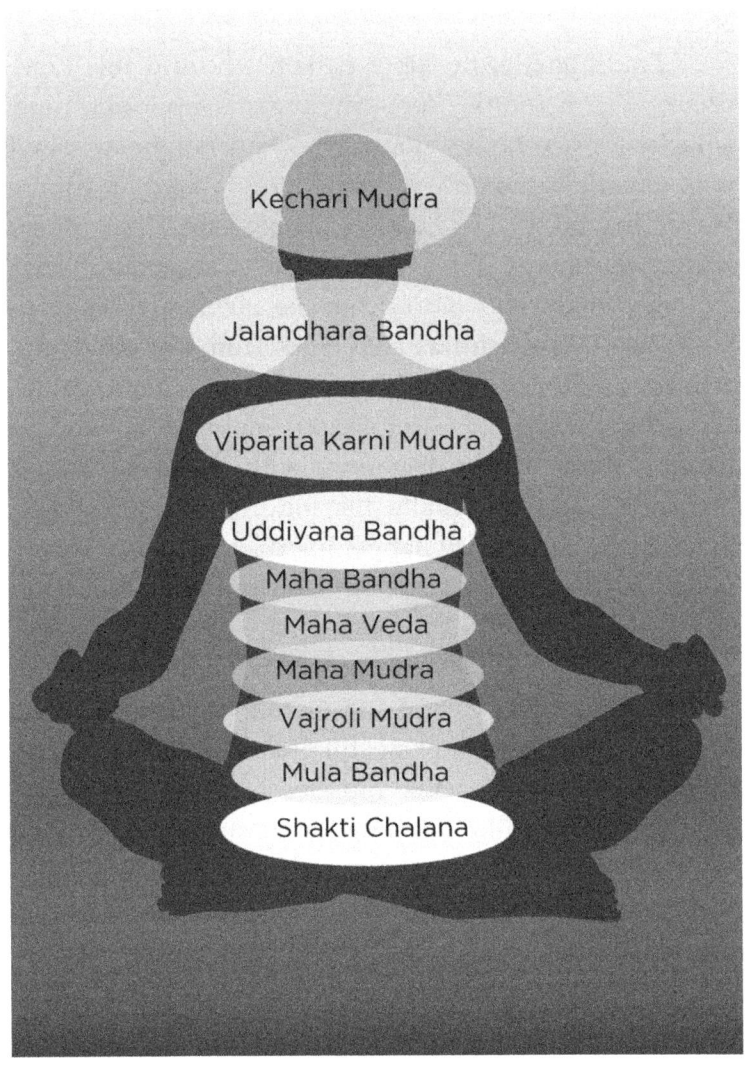

In this process of enlivening the organs up the trunk of the body into the throat, into the tongue, up into the head, becoming fully alive at each level, **a psychological and emotional churning happens.** The ancient yogis referred to this churning as *chalana*.

First, there is the churning of allowing each part of the body to be free in order for it to become enlivened. If a practitioner carries armor in the belly and the abdominal rectus muscle becomes fully alive, the armor gets thrown off. Then the practitioner has the unnerving experience of being free of armor and feeling all that it brings up to be vulnerable and exposed. The inclination is to struggle to get the armor back, but we have the option of practicing letting it go.

Then there is the churning generated by the inner conflict of whether to reestablish the armor or not. This might generate shame, attraction, or associations with past experiences. The key is recognizing that the current situation is not the past experience. It's similar enough to bring up old stuff, but it's new. We gain clarity and integration when we can let the stuff be there and not react to it.

Yoganand

Many years ago, I knew of a woman who had been a very devout Catholic, attending communion three times a day. Her husband was a lay brother in the church, and their whole lives revolved around the church. In her very first yoga class, the group was led in pranayama. She went very deep inside and then burst into several spontaneous postures before she collapsed in relaxation. The class went on, as the teacher watched her out of the corner of his eye.

When the class was over, she was full of amazement. She said, "I was with God. It was incredible." As the days passed, she continued having these automatic, very deep meditation experiences from just a little bit of yoga practice. Because she had lived her whole life immersed in her spirituality, she had a huge charge of energy built up. One day, she went to her teacher and said, "I was doing the pranayama you taught me and the strangest thing happened. My pelvic floor and my belly just pulled up!" He replied, "There are yogis in India who work for years to experience energy awakening through the locks. You don't even know their names, and they are happening for you automatically."

If the work is done to build a charge, and the container is strong enough, the energy will move. It's almost like an electric arc jumping from one electrode to another. Here, the energy is the arc, and the electrodes are the mudras.

The locks are esoteric, and most people cannot relate to them, but practicing the three locks is an excellent starting point, as they are good preparation and they give the feeling of the mudras. Willful practice of the locks works well to generate introversion and concentration. Once again, however, the more energy and the bigger the charge behind them, the more powerful and absorbing they are.

This is the path of energy. If an asana has low energy, it is an exercise. If an asana has high energy, it is a mudra. Have you had days where you do a posture and nothing happens, and other days you do the same posture and it feels amazing? It's the energy behind it. Kripalu Yoga and Pranakriya Yoga are descended from traditions that focused on energy. The postures, pranayamas, and mudras were all vehicles to activate the energy. They are the paddles, and the energy is the ping pong ball.

The Mudras and Sushumna

Another model for the mudras says that the three locks or the 10 mudras are sushumna, the central channel or pathway of bliss within the body. Each mudra clears out a different section of the channel between the pelvis and the crown of the head.

Remember from Chapter 2 that the phrase "hatha yoga" combines "sun" ("ha"), "moon" ("tha"), and "union" ("yoga"). The sun resides in the pelvis and lower abdomen, and is a raging fire that burns intensely. The moon is calm, cool, and serene, the rational self that lives in the crown of the head. **Hatha yoga connects the passionate animal self with the cool, rational self.** The rational self tries to ignore the passionate self, hoping it will go away, so it can be serene. **Hatha yoga recognizes that we need both the animal self and the rational self to become fully alive.**

When we open a channel between the pelvis and the crown, connecting the animal self and the rational self, the sun and the moon, that channel is sushumna. **You could say that the three locks or the 10 mudras are the pathway of sushumna. Each mudra illuminates a specific segment of the channel.**

If there were a little person at the base of your spine who was trying to travel up to the crown, he could not get through because of all the tension, tightness, and dullness along the path. Because the road is too dark for him to traverse, he needs a flashlight. Shining the flashlight into the pelvis is Mula Bandha. Once the pelvis is illuminated, he shines the light up into the belly, and that is Uddiyana Bandha. He shines it up into the throat, and that is

Jalandhara Bandha. Some passages in the texts indicate that sushumna already exists within us, but it is kept in the dark; the mudras illuminate sushumna.

Other texts suggest that sushumna does not automatically exist, but is actually created by the mudras, as they clear out the channel from the pelvis to the crown. Whether the mudras create sushumna, or it is already there and they merely illumine it, does not matter; they are just models. **The ultimate goal of the mudras is to illuminate and enliven the whole body.**

When multiple locks are engaged, they sometimes create the feeling of a vacuum that rises through the core of the body, as if the stomach is pulling on the throat. It can feel scary at first, but that's a sign that the body is becoming fully alive. It's not the only sign; there are many ways that increased aliveness can show up. Think about the sensation of heart palpitations: You might be driving along, not thinking at all about your chest. There's only vagueness there. All of a sudden, you feel movement in your heart, and it's scary! You can feel your heart. You can feel its shape. You can feel its structure. That's fascinating. It can be frightening when vagueness is replaced by clarity.

Imagine that degree of perception in every part of your body. Imagine feeling every subtle movement throughout your entire trunk. Most of us only feel something in our stomachs when it's pain. What if your stomach could be an extremely blissful place? **There might be so much bliss that you would cry because it felt so good. That's what it feels like when energy is flowing freely through your system.**

CHAPTER EIGHT
WORKING WITH PRANAYAMA

A yogi's work with the asanas, pranayamas, shatkriyas, and mudras is a long-term relationship. Imagine being married for a week, saying to your spouse, "Let's make love tonight!," and hearing the response, "Nah, we've already done that." It doesn't work that way. You do it again and again and again. Hopefully, 30 years later, not only are you still doing it, but you are looking for new ways to do it, new aspects to explore, new ways of sharing.

Do not expect to master these techniques overnight. By their nature, they invite exploration. Sometimes the ability to accomplish any yogic practice is thwarted by psychological resistance. With Bhramari pranayama, for example, it is possible that subtle resistance will not allow the vibration to go to certain places. Sometimes we have to go as far as we can, and open to that. Then we often find we can go to another level. Through this exploration, you grow into the practice. **Through the layers upon layers, you build a relationship with the practice.** You do not complete it and move on. You do not *know* Bhramari or the locks. You have been *introduced* to Bhramari and the locks.

Yoganand

After more than three decades of practicing yoga, I am still learning about the locks. New stuff comes all the time. It is rich. I have all these friends, these lovers, whom I can explore. I dance with them, I play with them, and they unfold. The relationship unfolds.

Forget the high and the Prana buzz; the pranayamas are primarily tools to help us unfold, get our energy flowing, and potentially channel that energy toward greater healing, strengthening the container, and, eventually, dissolving ahankara.

In our relationship to the pranayamas and the locks, we are children. We must grow into maturity with them. **If you've been initiated into that process, then you have received what we wanted you to receive from this book.** We do not expect you to walk away with a mastery of this work—but look at all the little seeds we have planted. You could take any single technique and practice it for a while, even if it was simply the foundational practice of Dirgha pranayama. What would it be like to practice Dirgha for 10 minutes first thing in the morning? Right before bed or before your asana practice? During your asana practice? How does it feel to do Anuloma Viloma after Bhastrika? Bhramari after Kapalabhati? They can all feed each other. You come up with amazing combinations. There's so much richness to tap into.

As we mentioned earlier, some traditions will tell you, "This is the correct and only way to do Bhastrika, Kapalabhati, and Anuloma Viloma." "This is the only way to do the locks." They might offer three versions of Kapalabhati, but they discourage any deviation from their instructions.

Rather than one right way, it's more like a bell curve. The middle represents the way most people should practice the technique, and there are practitioners on either side of that center doing it slightly differently, in the way that best fits their individual needs at a given point in time. You can adjust it accordingly, working from a place of being true to yourself.

Yoganand

In ancient times, I think a lot of teachers did not trust their students, which is why they said "Only practice this way." Then they watched them closely because they might have too much fun and lose the integrity of the practice, or they might get distracted and hurt themselves, a totally appropriate concern. When you reach the level of being a deft practitioner, I encourage you to practice in what I think is a more true or real way, which is to experiment and explore.

Swami Kripalu advised that we start out with the technique, then shift to the energy. When I lead students in warm-ups for asana practice, I often have them stand with their feet wide apart and press their hips forward, out to the right, back, left, and forward again. Once they establish circles, I tell them to focus on breath and sensation: a shift from the technique to the energy.

With pranayama, the energy is most important. When you shift your attention to the energy, you find that varying the pranayama slightly alters its effects on your energy. It's like exploring micro-movements in an asana. You might notice that, if you slow down your Bhastrika for five or 10 rounds and then speed it up again, it generates a big current of energy. The challenge is to build your discrimination enough to use the energy appropriately rather than simply chasing a high. If you say, "I hate my job, so I do a bunch of Bhastrika and, when I go to work, it's not so bad," then you're missing the point. That is using the energy as a smokescreen to make an unbearable experience more tolerable.

Pranayama was created to make you more sensitive, so that the disconnects in your life feel more painful. Why would we want to feel more pain? Because we can put up with a dull ache. We will almost always choose a long, drawn-out, dull pain over a quick, sharp one. We feel emotional. We get sad. We feel lonely. If we feel the stinging of that loneliness for 10 or 15 minutes, without resisting it, it evolves into something else and is gone. Guaranteed. What we usually do instead is eat a pint of ice cream and have a bellyache for six or eight hours. **We choose a dull pain when we could feel the sharp one and have it be over.**

Pranayama is intended to increase sensitivity so we can actually see how much pain we are in. Then **we can choose to take responsibility for it and change it.** One option is to say, "I hate this job, but I make a lot of trips to the water fountain. I eat a lot of cookies. I play on the internet when no one is looking. I do all these little things that keep me from being aware of how painful it is." Then, at some point, you begin to feel like someone stole your life. Another option is to say, "You know what? I hate this job. Bye."

Now, there is nothing wrong with having a job we don't like or being someplace we don't want to be *if* we can accept the situation and give it meaning. "I don't love this job, but I found a way to view it as serving people and providing me with an opportunity to grow." That is very different from "I am trapped" or "I don't deserve better." **There are a lot of people in very unhappy situations— unhappy relationships, unhappy health situations, unhealthy financial situations—because they don't believe they deserve better. That's an ahankara that needs to be purified.**

Pranayama is not meant to comfort or console. In images of the goddess Kali, who represents Prana, she does not hold a warm blanket in her hand. She bears a weapon and a severed head. She loves her children so much that she will not let anything hurt them. If you evoke Mother Kali and she awakens, she will look at you and say, "That addiction is draining your life. It's gone." "That relationship is not working for you. It's gone." You say "No, no, just a minute. I didn't want that. Why don't you go away, and I'll call you again next time?" But Kali does not work that way.

Prana is like Kali. If you do not want to grow, do not try to awaken Prana. If you do not want to be fully alive, do not try to awaken Prana. If you can develop enough discrimination, however, you can play with Prana. You can grow, heal, enliven and experience a level of personal freedom beyond anything you've ever imagined possible.

The Hindu Goddess Kali

One of the classical books on hatha yoga, the *Gheranda Samhita*, casts pranayama in the following light: "Now I shall tell thee the rules of pranayama, or regulation of breath. By its practice, a man becomes like a god." The term "god" here refers to an angelic being or a being of light. In other words, the yogi becomes a radiant being, living in a larger sphere with the ability to go places that ordinary people do not go, experiencing utter bliss and communion beyond that which ordinary people encounter.

This is all available to you. The bottom line is to be safe and to be true to yourself.

APPENDIX

DAILY PRANAYAMA PRACTICE PLANS

Throughout this text, we state that pranayama is not an exact science but more of a personal exploration. However, for those who want a clear starting point or road map, this appendix provides concrete direction for practicing pranayama.

First, we highly recommend practicing with guidance. It's extremely helpful to be guided in learning and practicing these techniques, especially for beginners. Yoganand has a pranayama CD, *Pranayama: The Pranakriya Approach To Yogic Breathing,* which can be purchased, both in hard copy and MP3 format, at Pranakriya.com. Allison offers free yoga resources, including several guided pranayama experiences, at AllisonGemmelLaframboise.com. Her yoga CD, *Bringing up the Sun,* also available on her website, includes a basic pranayama practice leading into the guided posture flow.

The practice plans that follow are meant to be used after you have learned the techniques. These plans are starting points. Explore how your body and its energies are affected by the pranayamas. Remember, if a technique doesn't feel good, don't practice it. Go back to more basic techniques for a while, then consider trying the challenging ones again.

With any of the practice plans provided for a given week, feel free to stay with it longer than a week if that feels appropriate. You could stay with Week 1 indefinitely if it feels right to you. Move onto the next week's plan when and if you feel ready. To modify, you can adjust the times for each pranayama or the number of rounds or expulsions.

Beginner's Practice Plan

Week 1

- Dirgha and Ujjayi – 5 minutes
- Basic Kapalabhati – 2 rounds of 30 expulsions each, no breath retention
- Meditation – 5 minutes

Week 2

- Dirgha and Ujjayi – 5 minutes
- Basic Kapalabhati – 2 rounds of 30 expulsions each, with external, then internal breath retention
- Nadi Shodhana (Anuloma Viloma without holding) – 8 minutes
- Meditation – 5 minutes

Week 3

- Dirgha and Ujjayi – 5 minutes
- Kapalabhati with external, then internal breath retention – two rounds of 30 expulsions each
- Single-Nostril Kapalabhati with external, then internal breath retention – two rounds on each side (left, right, left, right), 30 expulsions in each round
- Nadi Shodhana (Anuloma Viloma without holding) – 8 minutes
- Meditation – 5 minutes

Week 4

- Dirgha and Ujjayi – 5 minutes
- Kapalabhati with external, then internal breath retention – two rounds of 30 expulsions each
- Single-Nostril Kapalabhati with external, then internal breath retention – two rounds on each side (left, right, left, right), 30 expulsions in each round
- Alternate-Nostril Kapalabhati with external, then internal breath retention – two rounds of 40 expulsions each
- Nadi Shodhana (Anuloma Viloma without holding) – 8 minutes
- Meditation – 5 minutes

Week 5 and beyond

- Dirgha and Ujjayi – 5 minutes
- Kapalabhati with external, then internal breath retention – two rounds of 30 expulsions each
- Single-Nostril Kapalabhati with external, then internal breath retention – two rounds on each side (left, right, left, right), 30 expulsions in each round
- Alternate-Nostril Kapalabhati with external, then internal breath retention – two rounds of 40 expulsions each
- Nadi Shodhana (Anuloma Viloma without holding) – 2 minutes
- Anuloma Viloma – 10 minutes
- Meditation – 5 minutes

Intermediate Practice Plan

Week 1

- Dirgha and Ujjayi – 5 minutes
- Kapalabhati with external, then internal breath retention – two rounds of 50 expulsions each
- Single-Nostril Kapalabhati with external, then internal breath retention – two rounds on each side (left, right, left, right), 50 expulsions in each round
- Alternate-Nostril Kapalabhati with external, then internal breath retention – two rounds of 50 expulsions each
- Nadi Shodhana (Anuloma Viloma without holding) – 2 minutes
- Anuloma Viloma – 10 minutes
- Meditation – 5 minutes

Week 2

- Dirgha and Ujjayi – 5 minutes
- Kapalabhati with external, then internal breath retention – two rounds of 50 expulsions each
- Alternate-Nostril Kapalabhati with external, then internal breath retention – two rounds of 50 expulsions each
- Bhastrika with external, then internal breath retention – two rounds of 30 expulsions each
- Nadi Shodhana (Anuloma Viloma without holding) – 2 minutes
- Anuloma Viloma – 10 minutes

- Meditation – 5 minutes

Week 3

- Dirgha and Ujjayi – 5 minutes
- Kapalabhati with external, then internal breath retention – two rounds of 50 expulsions each
- Alternate-Nostril Kapalabhati with external, then internal breath retention – two rounds of 50 expulsions each
- Bhastrika with external, then internal breath retention – two rounds of 30 expulsions each
- Nadi Shodhana (Anuloma Viloma without holding) – 2 minutes
- Anuloma Viloma – 10 minutes
- Shitali or Sitkari – 5 minutes
- Meditation – 5 to 30 minutes

Week 4

- Dirgha and Ujjayi – 5 minutes
- Kapalabhati with external, then internal breath retention – two rounds of 50 expulsions each
- Alternate-Nostril Kapalabhati with external, then internal breath retention – two rounds of 50 expulsions each
- Bhastrika with external, then internal breath retention – two rounds of 30 expulsions each
- Nadi Shodhana (Anuloma Viloma without holding) – 2 minutes
- Anuloma Viloma – 10 minutes
- Bhramari – 5 minutes

- Meditation – 5 to 30 minutes

Week 5 and beyond

You can stay with the practice plan for Week 4 for as long as feels comfortable. If you want to take it further, you can add more expulsions to Kapalabhati or Bhastrika. You can also increase the length of time you practice Anuloma Viloma.

Basic Meditative Practice

- Dirgha and Ujjayi – 5 minutes
- Nadi Shodhana (Anuloma Viloma without holding) – 5 minutes
- Meditation or Relaxation – 5 minutes

Basic Energizing Practice

- Dirgha and Ujjayi – 5 minutes
- Kapalabhati with external, then internal breath retention – two rounds of 50 expulsions each
- Alternate-Nostril Kapalabhati with external, then internal breath retention – two rounds of 50 expulsions each
- Transition to a posture flow
- Finish with relaxation

ACKNOWLEDGMENTS

I am eternally grateful to my husband, Shaun, for being my backbone throughout this and all endeavors. You are a true life partner, and this book would not be complete without you. You have kept me on task, encouraged me, inspired me, and, above all, believed in me. Everyone needs a f*cking manager, and I am so thankful you are mine.

And to my children, Kai and Tayo, for breaking me wide open and allowing me to experience the farthest realms of myself.

Immense gratitude to my family for being a bedrock of support my entire life, providing me a foundation of truly unconditional love from which to leap. Thank you, Robbie, for taking me on that fateful yoga retreat in Costa Rica, for encouraging me to get into yoga, and for knowing me well enough to know I'd never return from Kripalu.

Thank you to Kripalu Center for Yoga & Health for being a crucible for the most incredible, transformational work I have ever experienced.

And to all those at Pranakriya who are spreading the invaluable teachings of Yoganand and Swami Kripalu; to Tresca Weinstein for her keen skills and support; to John M. for telling me I was a good writer and for firing me.

Heartfelt reverence to Swami Kripalu for being an essential figure in my lineage of yoga teachers and for the infinite ripples from his sincere exploration and unfolding.

Humble and deep gratitude to Yoganand for sharing this vast wisdom that made me want to write a book, for having faith in me to do this work justice, for his authenticity and dedication, and, most of all, for being my teacher.   —*AMGL*

Yoganand Michael Carroll, E-RYT500

Born into a strict fundamentalist Christian family, Yoganand left this religious tradition behind at age 16. Yoga—in particular the yoga of Swami Kripalu—offered him another way to channel the dedication to spirituality with which he was raised. He studied with Kripalu Yoga masters in India and the United States, and taught at Kripalu for more than 15 years before founding the Pranakriya™ School of Yoga Healing Arts. At the time of this printing, Yoganand is Dean of the Kripalu School of Yoga, leads Pranakriya Yoga teacher trainings and other programs around the country, and is a member of the International Association of Yoga Therapists. He is a masterful storyteller—through many years of intensive study and practice, he has gained a profound ability to distill and interpret esoteric yoga texts and techniques, making complex philosophical concepts accessible and engaging. When he's at home in South Florida, Yoganand spends time cultivating his collection of close to 500 orchids, whose ability to blossom and thrive in harsh environments amazes and inspires him.

For workshops with Yoganand, go to Kripalu.org and Pranakriya.com

Allison Gemmel Laframboise, E-RYT 500

Allison discovered yoga in college when she was both curious about the practice and looking for a way to ground herself through challenging life events. Seven years later, in 2003, she trained with Yoganand to become a yoga teacher at Kripalu Center for Yoga & Health. She has since studied with Yoganand and other renowned teachers in numerous depth trainings, and holds a professional-level teaching certification. Allison graduated Phi Beta Kappa from Boston University and has experience in psychology and public health research. Today her work is a combination of her life's true callings—teaching yoga and African-style hand drumming; running her yoga-inspired jewelry line, Prasada; helping to manage the yoga team at Kripalu; and her greatest passion of all, mothering her sons, Kai and Tayo. Allison is calmed, energized, and renewed by living on a lake in the Berkshires of western Massachusetts, where she loves to spend time enjoying life with her family. Once her boys are a bit older, she plans to get back to hobbies like playing piano and guitar, snowboarding, and waterskiing.

For workshops, blog and free yoga resources from Allison, go to AllisonGemmelLaframboise.com

RESOURCES

Kripalu.org – Kripalu Center for Yoga & Health. Retreats, workshops, trainings and general information about Kripalu. Includes workshops led by Yoganand and Allison.

Pranakriya.com – Pranakriya School for Yoga Healing Arts. Retreats, workshops, trainings and general information about Pranakriya Yoga. Includes workshops led by Yoganand.

AllisonGemmelLaframboise.com – Allison's blog and Free Yoga Resources, including guided pranayama experiences.

YogaAndDrumming.com – Yoga and Drumming Retreats with Allison and Shaun Laframboise.

PrasadaJewelry.com – Allison's yoga-inspired jewelry line. A portion of profits go to Kripalu's Teaching for Diversity program.

Made in the USA
Las Vegas, NV
27 September 2021